Good Work If You Can Get It

Good Work If You Can Get It

How to Succeed in Academia

JASON BRENNAN

JOHNS HOPKINS UNIVERSITY PRESS | *Baltimore*

Johns Hopkins Paperback edition, 2022
9 8 7 6 5 4 3 2 1

Johns Hopkins University Press
2715 North Charles Street
Baltimore, Maryland 21218-4363
www.press.jhu.edu

The Library of Congress has cataloged the hardcover edition of this
book as follows:

Names: Brennan, Jason, 1979– author.
Title: Good work if you can get it : how to succeed in academia /
    Jason Brennan.
Description: Baltimore : Johns Hopkins University Press, 2020. |
    Includes bibliographical references and index.
Identifiers: LCCN 2019033937 | ISBN 9781421437965 (hardcover) |
    ISBN 9781421437972 (ebook)
Subjects: LCSH: College teachers—Vocational guidance—United States. |
    College teaching—United States. | College teachers—Supply and
    demand—United States.
Classification: LCC LB1778.2 .B74 2020 | DDC 378.1/25023—dc23
LC record available at https://lccn.loc.gov/2019033937

A catalog record for this book is available from the British Library.

ISBN 9781421443287 (paperback)

Special discounts are available for bulk purchases of this book.
For more information, please contact Special Sales at
specialsales@jh.edu.

CONTENTS

Good Work If You Can Get It

Unpleasant Truths about the World's Best Job

THIS YEAR, some 1.7 million students will enroll full time in graduate school in the United States. Almost 80,000 will begin pursuing a PhD. The United States will award around 65,000 new doctoral degrees. In the humanities and social sciences, at least, the majority of new PhD students say they want to get work as professors.[1]

Most are destined for disappointment.

Roughly half will quit or otherwise fail to earn their doctoral degree. Most graduates will not get a full-time academic job of any sort upon graduation.[2] Only about 20% of students who start a PhD program will ever obtain a full-time faculty position, let alone a "good" professorship.[3]

The kinds of people who pursue a PhD have good analytical skills. They know how to collect and process data. Despite that, many would-be professors are clueless, naïve, and misinformed about what graduate school and academia are really like.

This book aims to fix that. It is a no-punches-pulled, frank, data-driven book telling you what academic life is like and what it takes to succeed in academia. I aim to help you succeed and also help you decide whether success is worth pursuing.

Two Booths

You may have seen a viral comic that shows two booths side by side. One booth offers "Unpleasant Truths." The other offers "Comforting Lies." Hundreds queue before the comforting lies. The unpleasant truths booth is empty.

You get the idea. Sometimes we want to evade reality. People would rather maintain a happy illusion. Indeed, there's a large body of research in psychology, economics, and political science investigating just when and why people indulge false beliefs.[4]

In some situations, you can't help but face the facts. If you're crossing the street, you'd better look both ways. You don't dare indulge the belief that you are a secret superhero impervious to damage. The nice—or gruesome—thing about traffic is that it disciplines you to accept and understand reality.

In other cases, however, you can put off dealing with the facts. The feedback comes later or is disconnected from one's individual inputs. Consider the parents who don't vaccinate their kids; since most other kids are vaccinated, most unvaccinated kids won't get sick. Think of a fifteen-year-old considering smoking at a party. He's tempted to indulge some illusions—that smoking isn't as bad as people say, that this is a one-time thing and he won't get addicted, that he'll be able to quit—because the harms come much later, when it's too late. Or think of a person deciding whether and how much to save for retirement. In the long run, saving now makes a huge difference, but the payoff comes decades later. Every year, she can convince herself it's safe to buy some extra toys and "make up for it" by saving more next year.

Attending graduate school is more like taking up smoking or choosing retirement plans than it is like crossing the street. Which field you study, which university you attend, how you spend your time, and so on, have huge effects on your career prospects. Some students enter graduate school with zero chance of obtaining good academic jobs. They are doomed on day one. But the penalty or reward comes five to fifteen years later.

Many potential and current PhD students remain uninformed about what their chances are really like or what it takes to beat the odds. Their professors—their advisors—are often just as bad. Indeed, professors have a perverse *incentive* to overstate their students' chances of success. Your grad school mentors want you to succeed, but they also want to maintain a PhD program for other reasons. Having graduate students increases professors' pay and provides them with graders and research assistants.[5] This means you can't always take your professors' advice at face value.

Consider this book the Unpleasant Truths booth about graduate school and academic life. But I mean to emphasize "truths" rather than "unpleasant." My goal is to answer your questions—plus the questions you don't yet know enough to ask—about what grad school is like, what it takes to get a job in academia, and whether a job in academia is even worthwhile.

These questions include: What should I know in deciding whether to go to graduate school? What kinds of jobs are there, and who gets them? What do people do in graduate school? What does it take to be productive, to publish continually at a high level? What does it take to teach many classes at once and manage grading, advising, and service? Are professors happy? What do they actually do with their time? What does it take to succeed in graduate school? How do I reduce or eliminate stress as an academic? How much does a PhD cost—and should I pay for one? How does "publish or perish" work? What is the difference between tenure-track, full-time but non-tenure-track jobs, and adjunct professorships? What are the differences between working at community colleges, liberal arts schools, or research universities? How much do professors get paid—and what's the distribution of income, benefits, and status? What do search committees look for—and what turns them off? Are academics hostile to and discriminatory against conservatives? How many jobs are there, and what are my chances? What does it take to beat the odds? Are some fields safer bets than others? How likely is it that jobs will disappear in the face of competition from MOOCs (massive open online courses) and online resources? How much do rankings matter? Will graduate school actually prepare me to be a professor? Is it safe to date other graduate students? How do I balance work and life?

When answering these questions, I won't be cynical, but I will be realistic. I won't exaggerate the upsides or the downsides of academic life. I'll tell you how it is, and as much as possible, I'll back up what I say with data and empirical studies. You won't like many of the answers, but you'll be better off knowing them. Misinformation can cause you to waste five to twenty years of your life. Good information can give you an edge.

I am not endorsing the current market conditions or saying that the system is good and just—indeed, I wrote an entire book arguing that academia has pervasive moral failings. You may frequently react to my advice by saying, "That's unfair!" You may be right. This book is not a call for a reform or a validation of the status quo. Rather, it's a guidebook for what it takes to succeed in academia as academia is, rather than a book discussing how academia *ought* to be.

Why Should You Listen to Me?

Qualifications matter. So, briefly, here are mine. I've published significant academic work on the political economy and business ethics issues of higher education, including the job market.[6] I've seen the market from all sides, and I've done so recently. In 2007, I was a postdoctoral research fellow and newly minted PhD; today, in 2019, as I write this sentence, I'm a tenured full professor holding a named chair. My experiences aren't stale or out of date. My experience of the academic market is post-financial crisis. It's the same as yours would be.

Though my name is on the cover, this book is coauthored in a way. I've spent a great deal of time discussing all these issues with my academic friends at a wide range of institutions, from small liberal arts colleges to giant research universities. Before I ever went on the market as a grad student, I attended professionalization seminars and strategy talks led by leaders such as Duke political scientist/economist Mike Munger, University of Arizona philosopher David Schmidtz, George Mason University economist Tyler Cowen, and Brown University political theorist John Tomasi. Many of the best ideas in this book ultimately come from them.

On "Quit Lit"

The *Chronicle of Higher Education*, *Inside Higher Ed*, and other magazines that cover higher ed frequently publish "Quit Lit" profiles of struggling academics who didn't make it. You should read these carefully. These articles are instructive, though often not in the way the authors intended.

Quit lit authors often express a sense of helplessness, as if academia is capriciously unfair, and there is nothing they could have done—or you could do—about it. That's misleading. Maybe academia is beset by structural injustices that you can't fix. But the choices you make—whether you study a field with a bad job market, whether you attend a high-ranked program or not, whether you dedicate your time in grad school to publishing or activism, whether you aim for prestigious journals or no-name publications—have a large effect on your job prospects.

Quit lit often presents the job market as if it were a lottery. Academia is not a perfect meritocracy, but it's not a lottery, either. The winners understand the system; the losers tend to make the same basic mistakes over and over again. My goal here is to help readers understand why the winners win, and the losers lose.

Taking Your Best Shot

If you're like most outsiders I've met, you picture academic life as genteel and quaint, removed from the rat race of corporate or government life. Academia is intense but low pressure.

Today, academia isn't like that; I don't know if it ever was. Success today requires hitting the ground running, starting the first day of grad school. You must professionalize right away and seek every distinction you can. You must be strategic and calculating. Maybe that's too bad—maybe grad school shouldn't be like that—but that's how it is.

Even if academia doesn't match your ideal, it's still a great gig, especially if you keep the job in its proper place. Academia is good work, *if you can get it*.

If you can get it. Let's work on that.

ONE

Do You Really Want an Academic Job?

Before You Start the Journey, Know the Destination

IT'S MY FIRST SEMESTER of graduate school. I'm sitting in the TA (teaching assistant) office. I start chatting with an older graduate student—let's call him "Ed"—who shares the office. Ed says, "I hate teaching. I hate writing papers. I just want to spend my time thinking about philosophy."

I laughed. He didn't like that. Turns out he wasn't kidding. In academia, teaching and writing papers *are the job*. Ed was like an athlete training full time for a sport he hated. If Ed just wanted to think about philosophy, he could have done so in his spare time. He could have held a better paying, less risky, more enjoyable job.

I've met many graduate students just like Ed. Many undergrads considering grad school are also like Ed. Some don't understand academic life or what professors do. Some see grad school as a way to kill time while they overcome some quarter-life crisis. Some people pursue a PhD because they couldn't think of anything else to do. Some are infatuated with cultivating an intellectual self-image. These are all silly reasons to get a PhD.

Think of an analogy to baseball. It makes little sense to start baseball training full time unless you enjoy the sport. You'd want to know what the game and the job are like, how much money players make and how they support themselves, whether they are happy, and so on. You'd also want to know the odds. How many people who start playing baseball manage to compete at the highest level? (Various websites I examined claimed the number of high school varsity baseball players who ever play a single major league baseball game range from 1 in 3,000 to 1 in 16,000.)

All this is also true for academia. Later chapters examine how to succeed in graduate school and as a professor. This chapter is meant to help you decide—given your values and your risk tolerance—whether you should even take a shot. I give you a thorough and frank account of what academic life is like. I start by laying out the landscape of academia. I talk about the different kinds of faculty jobs and the pay and status that attach to them. I describe what it's really like to be a professor. And I give you the basic odds of getting each kind of job.

What the PhD Is For

The PhD is a *professional* degree, like an MBA, a JD, or an MD. It is not designed for self-discovery, self-development, or personal enrichment. Maybe you'll get those things along the way, but that's not the point. (For what it's worth, though, various studies claim that graduate students suffer from high rates of anxiety and depression.)[1]

The PhD is designed to produce *new academic faculty*. To a lesser extent, it's designed to create nonacademic researchers for private or government jobs. If you get a PhD in engineering, economics, mathematics, statistics, or some of the natural sciences, there's a decent chance you can land a lucrative nonacademic research job. In most fields, there is little chance you'll find a research job outside of academia. However, as I discuss briefly in the conclusion, most PhDs eventually find a long-term full-time job, even if not in academia.

Given that PhD programs are generally designed and administered with the goal of producing new faculty, the typical program is rather poorly designed. There is little congruence between what most PhD programs train you to do and what most professors in fact do. The PhD primarily trains you to do research—to write original papers and conduct original experiments in your field. But, as you'll soon see, most faculty do little research and instead spend most of their time teaching or performing "service" work. Only a minority of professors spend the majority of their time doing research. Only a minority produce significant amounts of research—or research that is itself of much significance—over their careers. Many PhD programs provide little formal training in teaching. Nevertheless, the graduate students with the best research potential receive the most attention and respect.

There are more than three thousand four-year colleges and another sixteen hundred two-year colleges in the United States.[2] A minority of these have active doctoral programs, which regularly produce new researchers and college faculty. If you go to graduate school, your professors/mentors/advisors will be among the rare few professors who work in research-oriented universities and actively produce new research. This is a major reason why many graduate students get misleading advice about success in academia from their mentors: their mentors have *unusual* academic jobs.

Graduate school professors tend to train their students for the jobs *they* have. They train students to work as tenure-track professors at research-intensive doctoral universities. But statistically speaking, most PhDs won't get that kind of job. For instance, the 35th-ranked philosophy department at Georgetown University has a pretty good placement rate. Most Georgetown philosophy PhDs secure some sort of tenure-track professorship. Still, over the past decade, only one graduate out of thirty-two has landed a research-intensive position in which she spends most of her time creating new knowledge.[3] The rest are full-time college teachers.

A Week in the Lives . . .

Do you want to be a professor? One way to determine that is to look at how representative professors from different kinds of universities or colleges spend their typical work weeks. Higher education is not all one thing, especially from the perspective of faculty. Some universities primarily focus on teaching undergraduates, while some focus on teaching graduate (master's or doctoral) students. Some focus on teaching, period, while a few focus on producing original research.

The Carnegie Commission categorizes colleges and universities into types. We don't need to go through each type at length here. Instead, let's focus on four main categories:

1 Research I, or "R1," universities are universities that grant a high number of PhDs or other research doctorates and that produce the highest levels of research. Examples include the Ivy League schools, MIT, Johns Hopkins, Michigan, Duke, Georgetown (my employer), UCLA and Berkeley, UNC Chapel Hill, Stanford.

2 R2 and R3 universities grant fewer doctoral degrees and produce less research. Think Ball State University, University of North Carolina at Greensboro, Central Michigan University, Rochester Institute of Technology.

3 Liberal arts colleges and regional colleges and universities do not grant doctoral degrees but instead focus on baccalaureate education.

4 Community colleges have open-admissions policies and focus on remedial education, trade education, or basic liberal arts education leading to the associate's degree.

R1 Universities

At R1 universities—universities with the "highest research activity"—faculty members face constant pressure to publish, but they also enjoy radical freedom, with a daily schedule that's largely up to them. I work at an R1, so I'll use my own experiences as an illustration.

Tenure-track faculty at R1s usually teach four or fewer classes a year. For me, this means that I spend less than four hours in a classroom per week per semester. I teach either one or two classes per semester, no more than three classes a year. I teach on Mondays and Wednesdays only; I have Tuesdays, Thursdays, and Fridays free. Occasionally, I must spend a few hours grading papers or preparing lectures. However, by design—to free up research time—I largely teach the same classes each semester. Thus, many semesters I need do *no* new or additional preparation to teach a class. Most years, I spend about two hundred hours a year on teaching-related activities, including 135 hours in class and about 65 outside of class.

When I worked at Brown, graduate teaching assistants did most of my grading for me. Despite having three hundred or so students a year, I could go an entire year without reading or grading an undergraduate student paper, if I so desired.

On most Tuesdays, Thursdays, and Fridays, I work from home, working on whatever project I please. Most days, I wake up, work out, and then spend five hours writing whatever I feel like writing. In a typical week, I have maybe five hours of "scheduled work," such as attending a committee meeting, meeting with students, or listening to a guest lecture. The other thirty-five hours of my work are up to me.

Many weeks, I spend a night or two away to give a paid talk on my research somewhere else. That "somewhere else" could be anywhere in the world—at another university, a business, with a government consortium, or at a private foundation. I get invitations from all over the world. Some years I do thirty or more talks; some years I say no and keep it under ten. That's up to me, too.

I don't teach over the summer. As long as I publish, I get a "summer research bonus" worth two-ninths of my base salary. While I take a few vacations each summer, I also spend my summers how I spend the academic year: writing papers and books.

This is the life of a tenured, research-productive professor at an "R1: Doctoral University: Highest Research Activity" school. If I were a scientist, I'd probably spend my unscheduled time in my lab rather than in front of my laptop, but the deal is basically the same.

If you go to graduate school, especially a good one, your professors and mentors will mostly be like me and have my kind of lifestyle and work life. The problem for you, again, is that our idea of what academic life is may be provincial or narrow. We'll train you for our kind of job, even though most faculty don't have jobs like ours. Most students get a different kind of academic gig, if they get one at all.

R2 and R3 Universities

Let's peek at the work week of a typical tenure-track professor at a large, less research-intensive, more regional state university: Boise State.

A 2014 study of faculty life at Boise State University found that their average tenure-track faculty member works sixty-one hours a week. This includes about twenty-five hours per week in teaching and teaching-related activities.[4] And no wonder they spend so much time teaching: whereas R1 profs teach four or fewer courses a year, typical tenure-track Boise State professors teach three courses per semester. This can be reduced to two per semester if they get external research grants and oversee graduate students.[5]

According to the anthropologists who surveyed Boise State faculty,

> the most surprising finding of our analysis of practices was that faculty spent approximately 17 percent of their workweek days in meetings. These meetings included everything from advising meetings with students (which could be considered part of teaching or service depending on the department) to committee meetings that have a clear service function. Thirteen percent of the day was spent on email (with functions ranging from teaching to research and service). Thus, 30 percent of faculty time was spent on activities that are not traditionally thought of as part of the life of an academic. Twelve percent of the day was spent on instruction (actual lectures, labs, clinicals, etc.), and an equal amount of time was spent on class preparation. Eleven percent of the day was spent on course administration (grading, updating course web pages, etc.). Thus, 35 percent of workweek days was spent on activities traditionally thought of as teaching. Only three percent of our workweek day was spent on primary research and two percent on manuscript writing.[6]

The Carnegie Commission—a group that classifies colleges and universities into broad types based upon the kinds of degree they offer and the amount of research they produce—classifies Boise State University as an "R2," a "High Research

Activity Doctoral University."[7] This is just one step below R1 universities like Yale or Caltech. Nevertheless, average faculty at Boise State spend only 5% of their time doing research. The survey finds that faculty spend the majority of time—over 60%—working on campus. The rest is split between work at home and in other locations. The typical Boise State professor works on the weekends.

Boise State professors seem to be good representatives of life at R2s or R3s. A national survey from 2003 by the US Department of Education and another survey by the Higher Education Research Institute at UCLA also find that the average "research university" professor spends about twenty-four hours per week on teaching-related activities.[8] Once you drop out of the top fifty or so research universities, most professors dedicate most of their time to teaching and service, not research, so it's not surprising that most scholarship is produced by a small minority of faculty and that most faculty publish little or nothing in any given two-year period.

That's a snapshot of life at the R2s and R3s. You have larger teaching and service obligations but are still expected to produce original research. You're given less freedom, money, and time to do that research, though, and so you'll predictably produce less of it.

Liberal Arts Colleges and Regional Colleges and Universities

At liberal arts colleges or at regional colleges and universities, the work focus shifts even more toward teaching and service. For example, the 2003 Department of Education study finds that private liberal arts college faculty spend an average of thirty-six hours per week on teaching activities, or almost 66% of their typical workweek.[9] Some elite liberal arts colleges, such as Smith, Amherst, or Williams, expect faculty to produce high-quality research and give them the time and resources to do so. But at the typical small liberal arts school, professors focus on postsecondary teaching. At small liberal arts colleges, professors often teach four or five classes a semester. Many classes are "service" courses—lower-level classes that fulfill some general education requirement or that are necessary to complete an undergraduate major. Departments are often small. Faculty must often be able to teach any class the department offers, not just courses in their narrow specialty or related to their dissertation. The German professor's dissertation may focus on interpreting six troublesome pages of Kafka's *Die Abweisung*, but she'll spend most of her class time teaching German 101.

Further, faculty at liberal arts colleges—including and perhaps especially at the elite liberal arts colleges—are expected to make themselves available to students. They are encouraged to attend campus social events, to oversee and assist student clubs and organizations, to socialize informally with students, to advise students, and to keep their office doors open for impromptu student visits and discussions. Working from home is frowned upon. You should be around.

At small liberal arts colleges, tenure-track faculty must on occasion publish peer-reviewed research. Still, the focus is on teaching. An assistant professor at Indiana University may be expected to publish more original and important research in her first seven years than a professor at a small liberal arts college might publish in her entire career.

Liberal arts colleges are often highly dependent on tuition dollars. Their professors may face pressure to "put butts in seats"—to attract students to their major and keep students happy.

Community Colleges

At two-year community colleges, faculty do even more teaching and service. Most professors teach five introductory or remedial courses a semester; some teach even more.[10] They advise students, help run clubs, and provide tutoring outside of class. They usually have no research expectations at all.

Because there are no research expectations, in the past it was often possible to get a full-time tenure-track professorship at a community college with only a master's degree. However, that's changing fast. There is a glut of PhDs (see chapter 4). Community colleges that would have hired an MA/MS twenty years ago now want and can get PhDs for their long-term positions.

Keep in mind that I am not making any claims here about which kind of university is better or more valuable. I'm not saying that the typical jobs *should* be like this. Maybe R1 faculty should teach more while liberal arts college faculty should have more time for research. Again, my goal is to tell you what it's like, not how it should be.

The Academic Ranks

Academia is a weird world. Academics tend to be nerdy introverts, but job success is highly dependent on networking. Academics tend to be left-wing egalitarians,[11] but academia itself is hierarchical. Everything gets ranked, including universities themselves, individual graduate departments, and book and journal publishers in individual academic fields. Faculty spend lots of time fretting over rank and status.

Undergraduate students call anyone in front of the class "professor." They think "professor" = college teacher. That's not quite right—sometimes the college teachers are PhD students working as teaching assistants or instructors of record.

Sometimes academic administrators teach classes. Sometimes the people teaching are long-term, full-time teaching faculty but don't have the word "professor" in their titles. There's a wide variety of type and rank of professor. The table below categorizes faculty by status, contract type, contract length, and rank. It also roughly shows career progression and ranks. Moving down the column means moving up in rank, power, prestige, and pay. The left side of the table has more rank, power, prestige, and pay than the right, with the exception of the visiting associate and visiting full professor positions.

Types and ranks of academic jobs

	Long-Term		Short-Term	
Tenure-Track	*Non-Tenure-Track*		*Full-Time*	*Part-Time*
	Research track	*Teaching track*		
Assistant professor (untenured but tenure eligible)	Assistant research professor	Instructor, assistant teaching professor	Visiting assistant professor (VAP)	Adjunct professor (adjunct)
Associate professor (tenured)	Associate research professor	Lecturer, associate teaching professor	Postdoctoral research fellow (postdoc)	
(Full) professor (tenured)	(Full) research professor	Senior lecturer, teaching professor, clinical professor, professor of the practice	Visiting associate professor	
Endowed chair/ university professor/ distinguished (full) professor (tenured)	Distinguished (full) research professor	Distinguished teaching professor, distinguished professor of the practice	Visiting professor	

Not every American or Canadian university uses the same exact titles or rankings, but most follow something close to what's shown in the table. However, note that British, Irish, Australian, and various other international universities may have entirely different ranks or use the same label in different ways. For instance, a "lecturer" in the United States is a non-tenure-track teaching professor, but in the United Kingdom a lecturer is the equivalent of the US or Canadian tenure-track assistant professor. In the UK, "professor" is often the equivalent to an endowed chair in the US.

Note that the "assistant" moniker just means "less than associate." Assistant professors don't actually *assist* the senior professors, at least not in North America.

The Tenure Track

The gold standard faculty job is the tenure-track professorship. To be on the tenure track means that your job is eligible for tenure. Tenure is an up or out system. Tenure-track faculty are hired as assistant professors for a six- or seven-year probationary period. At the end of that time, they apply for tenure. If they fail, they get *fired*.[12] If they succeed, they are promoted to associate professor and granted tenure.

The short probationary period may seem harsh, but it's actually something faculty lobbying groups fought for. It's meant to protect faculty, not create a pretext for firing them. In the past, universities could string assistant professors along forever without making a tenure decision. The current system is meant to stop that.

Having tenure means that a faculty member can be fired only for "cause," such as serious dereliction of duty, serious violations of university policy, or when the university faces severe financial problems. In the last case, many universities are contractually obligated to lay off many non-tenure-track faculty, staff, and administrators before they may terminate any tenured faculty. However, university and college presidents tend to be crafty at circumventing these rules; they often succeed in firing tenured faculty in some low-demand program while keeping their bloated administrations full.[13]

The standards to earn tenure vary tremendously from university to university. At R1 universities, tenure is based almost entirely on research output. Faculty must publish a large number of peer-reviewed articles or books in whatever their academic field considers the best journal or book publishers.

At other places, tenure is based more on a combination of research, teaching performance, and service to the school and profession. At a small liberal arts college, you may only have to publish one or two peer-reviewed articles in second-tier journals, but you must be able to demonstrate excellence in teaching and significant innovation in service projects. (Deans commonly use student teaching evaluations to assess teaching excellence, even though most research finds these are invalid measures of teaching performance.)[14]

A law-abiding, rule-following tenured associate professor has a job for life. For that reason, tenure-track faculty are extremely expensive. Tenuring a professor is a high-risk activity, which commits a university to another twenty to thirty years of rising salary and benefit expenditures. Tenure-track faculty cannot be "repurposed" easily. If student enrollment drops in English but rises in economics, you can't switch the English profs over to the economics department, nor can you easily lay them off.

Once tenured, associate professors no longer have to "publish or perish." I work at an R1, yet I have tenured colleagues who haven't published any peer-reviewed research in a decade and who aren't even *trying* to publish. They don't do their jobs, but they won't lose their jobs.

The nominal reason for the tenure system is that tenured faculty have supposedly earned the freedom and right to work on long-term, high-impact, risky, and big ideas, rather than focusing on pumping out small articles year after year. To get tenure, assistant professors have to prove they can hit. Tenured faculty are now encouraged to hit home runs, to shoot for high-risk, big ideas. However, researchers in sociology and economics have studied whether tenure in fact induces faculty to "swing for the fences." It turns out—as you might expect—that tenured faculty usually become lazier, more boring, and less productive.[15] Big surprise.

If associate professors perform well, by continuing to publish or by exhibiting sustained excellence in teaching, they can apply for promotion to professor, or what people often call "full professor" (to distinguish from "assistant" or "associate" professors). This promotion comes with additional pay, perks, and status, but it also often comes with additional responsibility. Full professors are supposed to take the lead in faculty governance, internal merit evaluations, and so on.

In addition, select professors who perform at an extremely high level (by their university's standards) may receive an endowed/named chair, or equivalent title, such as "Distinguished Professor" or "University Professor" or something like "Romeo Elton Professor." This isn't an additional rank so much as an honorific. These titles often come with increased pay, research funding, or rights and privileges.

In general, at a given school, the tenure-track faculty have the highest status and power. They make the decisions about whom to hire and promote within their departments. They have full voting rights on faculty and university governance. They make the most money, get the best offices, march first in graduation ceremonies, and so on.

Long-Term Gigs outside the Tenure Track

Because hiring tenure-track faculty is so risky and expensive and because tenured faculty cannot be repurposed, most colleges and universities also maintain a parallel core of non-tenure-track but long-term faculty. Generally, such teaching faculty are expected to have a PhD or equivalent, though instructors and so-called professors of the practice sometimes have only a master's degree. (Professors of the practice are usually former professionals, such as lawyers or businesspeople, hired to teach the skills they used on the job.)

Some such faculty specialize in undergraduate instruction, advising, and curriculum development. At most schools, the career progression is instructor to lecturer to senior lecturer to distinguished senior lecturer. Some schools use different titles. The equivalent career progression might instead be assistant teaching professor, associate teaching professor, and then full or even distinguished teaching professor. In business or professional schools, such faculty may have titles like assistant/associate/(full) professor of the practice or assistant/associate/(full) clinical professor.

These professors typically receive lower salaries than the comparable tenure-track faculty in the same department. They generally lack voting rights, though they may have some power and say over undergraduate education. They have few or no research obligations, but they are expected to teach a heavier course load and do more service work than their tenure-track colleagues.

Although they are not tenure-eligible, these jobs tend to be secure. Faculty are often hired on rolling three- or five-year contracts, with every expectation that they will serve at the same university over their entire careers. They receive full benefits, perks, offices, computers, and are considered a real part of the faculty, despite often lacking the right to engage in faculty governance. If a university faces financial hardship and must fire faculty, it may be contractually obligated to fire the non-tenure-track faculty before firing any tenured faculty.

Some universities also maintain a core of non-tenure-track *research* faculty. They might be called clinical professors, or have a career progression of assistant research professor, associate research professor, (full) research professor, and even distinguished research professor. These professors are hired solely to do research—perhaps in a medical or physics laboratory—and have no teaching obligations.

Sometimes such research faculty have secure long-term jobs akin to their instructor/lecturer/senior lecturer counterparts. Sometimes—especially if they are funded by federal or foundational grants—they are hired with less expectation of long-term residence at the university. At any rate, their pay tends to be equal to or higher than that of the teaching-track faculty, in part because it is more difficult to find good, productive researchers than good, productive teachers. They are also considered real faculty members, albeit second class. They usually don't have voting rights in faculty governance.

Short-Term Jobs

The lowest status and lowest paid faculty jobs are *adjunct* teaching positions. Adjuncts earn a fee in exchange for preparing their classes, teaching, grading papers, and meeting with students. Adjuncts are contract workers, hired to teach a class. They generally have no job security. Their classes could be canceled at a moment's notice. There is no guarantee or expectation that they will be hired again next semester. They usually receive no benefits, no office, no research account, no computer, and no other perks. They're treated as if they are not "real faculty."

Teaching fees vary greatly. On average, across all colleges in the United States, adjuncts earn about $2,700 per course, or $3,100 per course if they have a doctorate.[16] Four-year colleges pay adjuncts more than that on average, while two-year colleges pay them less. Some universities—such as my own—are committed to paying adjuncts what they consider a living wage. Business schools and law schools often hire businesspeople and lawyers to teach classes on the side; these adjuncts can make tens of thousands for a single class. Humanities departments sometimes hire famous authors as adjuncts, while schools of government often hire famous politicians; again, these special-case adjuncts make far more than normal adjunct rates.

Most adjuncts lack a terminal degree; somewhere between 18% and 30% of them possess a doctorate.[17] A PhD or equivalent is a necessary prerequisite for a tenure-track or full-time appointment in most academic fields. Thus, most adjuncts are ineligible for a full-time faculty job.

Adjuncting is not an entry-level job into more lucrative full-time positions. The majority of adjuncts are instead graduate students teaching courses on the side (often at neighboring colleges), moonlighting professionals, or others with a master's degree or less.

You may have heard that universities have been replacing full-time faculty with adjuncts. US Department of Education statistics show these rumors to be false. In fact, the ratio of full-time professors to students has remained stable over the past forty-five years, at about 24:1.[18] It's true that among all colleges and universities in the United States, the ratio of adjuncts to full-time faculty is now about 50:50. However, this isn't because four- and two-year colleges have been replacing their full-timers with adjuncts. Instead, they've *added* adjuncts at a far faster rate than they've added full-time faculty.

(Again, the growth of full-time faculty has kept pace with student enrollments.) Indeed, much of the adjunct growth is driven by the for-profit educational sector, such as the University of Phoenix or Strayer University, which relies almost entirely on adjunct labor.[19]

Another step up the perk/status/pay ladder is the visiting assistant professor, or VAP. A VAP is usually a newly minted PhD hired to teach a full load of courses for a year or two. Colleges sometimes hire VAPs to cover another professor's classes while that professor has a sabbatical, or simply to cover extra classes the full-time faculty can't teach. A VAP is a teaching gig, not a research job.

The number of courses a VAP teaches depends upon the school, but it's generally equal to or greater than whatever a full-time tenure-track professor at that school would teach. Pay might be between $40,000 and $70,000 a year, plus benefits and perks. VAPs usually receive an office and might receive a small research or travel budget.

New PhDs who fail to get a full-time faculty job often take VAP jobs to remain in academia and earn money while they wait for the next hiring cycle. Some new PhDs string together different VAPs year after year, moving across the country each summer, hoping to get a permanent job the year after.

A postdoctoral research fellowship (postdoc) is a more prestigious temporary position. Postdocs usually last between one and four years. Postdocs might be expected to teach one or two classes a year, or to assist a senior, tenured faculty member in her laboratory. While senior faculty often have no meaningful interaction with the VAPs, these same professors actively mentor and support the postdocs.

The purpose of the postdoc is to cultivate new talent by giving new PhDs the time, space, and money to improve their research skills. Postdocs are encouraged to take an active part in departmental and university life.

While a postdoc isn't a permanent job, the combination of pay, freedom, time for research, networking, and mentoring is often so attractive that new PhDs will often turn down tenure-track jobs to take a postdoc at a more prestigious school. The visiting associate/full professor gigs are a special category. It's not as though postdocs or VAPs might get promoted into these jobs. Rather, universities often host tenured faculty from other universities. A professor on sabbatical might spend a year working at another school. Some universities have research centers that routinely hire tenured faculty from other universities to visit for a year. Visiting faculty go on leave from their home university for a year and then return.

Colleges and universities encourage this practice because the life of the mind requires intellectual exchanges and collaboration with new people. Departments also sometimes hire one-year visitors before offering those senior professors a permanent, tenured gig. The visiting professor and the host institution can determine if they're a good match.

How Many in Each Category?

You might wonder what percentage of faculty fits into each category. According to the US Department of Education, there were more than 800,000 full-time (i.e., tenured/tenure-track or permanent but non-tenure-track) faculty and about 730,000 part-time (i.e., mostly adjunct) faculty in the United States as of 2016, the most recent available year. For what it's worth, the number of full-time faculty has continued to grow over the past twenty years, while the total number of part-time faculty has declined since 2011.[20]

There is, therefore, nearly a 50:50 ratio of full-time to adjunct faculty across the United States. However, as I explained above, universities have not been replacing full-time faculty with part-time adjuncts. The ratio of full-time faculty to students has remained almost constant since 1970; it's actually better now than in 1987. Rather, the explosion of for-profit alternatives to traditional college produced a massive increase in the number of adjunct faculty around the country. At the same time, traditional two- and four-year colleges added large numbers of adjunct faculty—often to teach in their lucrative "continuing studies" programs, aimed at nontraditional students.

At public research universities across the United States, about 49% of faculty are tenure-track, 27% are full-time/long-term non-tenure-track, and 24.4% part time. At public teaching-focused universities, about 43% of faculty are tenure-track, 46% full-time/long-term non-tenure-track, and 11% part time. At private nonprofit research universities, the percentages are 40, 27, and 24. At private teaching-focused colleges, the percentages are 30, 18, and 53. At two-year colleges, both public and private, the overwhelming majority of faculty are part time.[21]

Nationwide, 33.5% of all professors are tenure-track, 50% are part-time, and the remainder are full-time, long-term but non-tenure-track professors. What this means is that over two-thirds of *full-time* professors are tenure-track, but only one-third of all professors (including the part-timers) are tenure-track. Again, the reason tenure-track faculty are a minority of the professoriate isn't that they're getting replaced by adjuncts, but that universities have added a huge number of adjuncts on top of the tenure-track faculty. Increases in full-time faculty have kept pace with student enrollments; increases in adjunct faculty have greatly exceeded student enrollments.

Show Me the Money!

Don't go into academia for the money.

If you're smart and conscientious enough to complete a PhD from a decent university, and if you're talented enough to have any real shot at even a mediocre faculty job, then you probably could make more money working in accounting, finance, law, or medicine. You'll also have better odds of getting any job, let alone a good job, in those fields. That said, the money's pretty good. Full-time professors tend to be squarely middle and upper-middle class.

In 2017, across *all* four-year colleges and universities in the United States, on average, full professors made $104,280, associate professors made $81,274, assistant professors made $70,791, and lecturers and instructors made between $55,000 and $60,000.[22]

Those are the averages, but there is tremendous variation in pay. Salary, benefits, and other income depend on (1) how rich the college or university is, (2) what kind of university or college it is, (3) which field the professor works in, and (4) how famous or important a particular professor is.

In general, elite doctorate-granting research universities pay their professors the most. Pay progressively decreases from there to non-elite doctoral universities, to master's-granting universities, to four-year-only colleges, and then finally to two-year colleges.

For instance, according to an American Association of University Professors (AAUP) report, in 2017–18, at doctoral universities, full professors at the 95th percentile of income made $205,860 in salary; at the 50th, $135,130; and at the 10th percentile, $106,579. Assistant professors at those universities at the 95th percentile made $115,201; at the 50th percentile, $85,534; and at the 10th, $70,853.

In contrast, at four-year-only colleges, full professors at the 95th percentile averaged $142,192; at the 50th percentile, $86,150; and at the 10th, $64,141. The numbers for assistant professors at four-year-only colleges: 95th percentile, $85,131; 50th percentile, $61,572; 10th percentile, $49,962.

At universities that grant master's degrees (but not doctorates), the pay is slightly higher than at four-year colleges. At community colleges, it's slightly lower.[23] The US Department of Education's published numbers are similar to the AAUP's.[24]

Further, the AAUP maintains a yearly survey of faculty salary and compensation, broken down by individual universities and colleges.[25] Professors at rich research universities make significantly more than others. The average Harvard full professor makes $245,000 in salary, while the average Harvard assistant professor makes a whopping $140,700.[26] If anything, Harvard's full professor figure is misleadingly *low*, because Harvard's academic ranks are slightly different from those at most other American schools. At Harvard, assistant professors are first promoted to associate professors without tenure, and then are promoted to full professors with tenure. So, the "full professor" rank at Harvard also includes people who would be the equivalent of younger, lower-paid associate professors elsewhere. What this means is that the best-paying university pays better than the numbers indicate.

Keep in mind that these numbers are for *salaries* only. Faculty also receive health insurance, dental insurance, life insurance, disability insurance, retirement benefits, tuition assistance/remission/discount programs, and a wide package of other benefits. These tend to be worth another third or more of faculty salary.[27] Furthermore, some faculty earn additional income by speaking, publishing, and consulting.

Remember, however, that many of the universities with the highest nominal salaries, such as Stanford or Columbia, are also in the most expensive parts of the country. Once you adjust for cost of living, $200,000 a year at Washington University, in St. Louis, is more money than $250,000 at Harvard or MIT, in Cambridge, Massachusetts.[28]

However, many of the richest universities, such as Columbia, NYU, and Princeton, also defray the high cost of living by providing subsidized housing for faculty or by offering mortgage assistance, grants, and low-cost loans for purchasing a home. In academia, the people at the top have it good.

In contrast, the median *household* (not individual) income in the United States in 2015 was about $59,039, whereas *mean* household income was about $72,000.[29] Thus, the median assistant professor at a four-year-only liberal arts college earns more money than the median US household and earns almost as much as the mean US household. Professors tend to be upper-middle class.

Income also depends on one's academic *field*. Brand new tenure-track assistant professors in business, computer science, engineering, and law tend to make about $30,000 more than professors in history, psychology, or English.[30] In general, the easier it is for you to get a high-paying job with your degree outside academia, the more you earn inside academia.

Income also depends on the individual professor. Universities must compete to hire and retain star professors. Famous professors in high demand make far more than others. Harvard pays John Bates Clark Medal–winner economist Roland Fryer more than $600,000 a year.[31] Some star medical and business school faculty receive multi-million-dollar salaries.[32]

In general, the more and better you publish, the more you make, regardless of whether you work at an R1 or a less research-oriented school. Even star humanities professors at elite schools can make well over $200,000 a year in their base salaries, plus also secure significant honoraria, speaking fees, and book royalties. When professors deliver guest lectures at other schools, some earn as little as $500. Nobel-laureate economists and bestselling authors can get $25,000 to $50,000 or more. Even at teaching-focused schools, the most research-productive professors tend to earn more than their colleagues.

Faculty generally receive 8%–15% of their book and textbook sales in royalties. Most faculty never publish a book, so they don't have access to royalty income. For most faculty who do publish the occasional book, royalties amount to a few hundred dollars every few years; there isn't a huge market for books on avant-garde seventeenth-century Romanian poetry, it turns out.

However, some professors make tens of thousands or even millions in royalties over their lifetimes. Harvard economist Greg Mankiw has sold more than a million copies of his popular (and excellent!) *Principles of Economics* textbook,[33] which sells for $181 on Amazon and for more in college bookstores. I don't know what his royalty rate is, but if he gets only the standard 10%, that's at least $18 million in royalties in current dollars.

In academia, money, fame, and freedom are tied to research, not teaching. I'll summarize this with an example Phil Magness and I use in *Cracks in the Ivory Tower*.

> Suppose Martha is a star researcher with a high citation count, who publishes major books or articles year after year, with legions of other researchers reading and responding to her work. But suppose Martha is a lousy teacher. Suppose Nate is an exceptional teacher, whose students love and cherish him. Nate can transform barely literate college freshmen into independent and creative thinkers. But suppose Nate rarely publishes, and no one reads what he writes.

How do their careers go? Martha will probably earn a base salary three to five times Nate's. She'll receive another $20–50K or so in speaking fees each year; Nate won't be invited anywhere. She'll end up working at a fancier and more prestigious university than Nate. She'll enjoy extensive freedom to set her schedule, while Nate will have his week filled with classes and service meetings. Martha may choose where in the world she lives and works, while Nate will be stuck living wherever he happened to land his first job.[34]

Keep in mind, I'm not making any judgments here. I'm not saying Martha is better, happier, or more deserving than Nate. I'm not claiming that she should get paid more or that Nate's work is less valuable. I'm not saying you should hope to be Martha rather than Nate. I'm just saying that this is how academia works: compensation, prestige, and freedom are tied more to research productivity than to teaching excellence.

What Are Your Chances of Getting a Full-Time Job?

So, now you've got a taste of what being a professor is like and what it pays. What are the chances you'll get a tenure-track job, or any job?

According to one peer-reviewed analysis, only about 12.8% of all PhD graduates in the United States can ever hope to land a tenure-track job. Fewer than 17% of all science PhD graduates find a tenure-track job within three years of graduating.[35] There isn't as good data on tenure rates, but it appears that at least half of tenure-track assistant professors eventually get tenure.[36]

While most colleges and universities focus on teaching rather than research, research-intensive universities tend to have larger faculties than small liberal arts colleges. As a result, as of 2011, the *Chronicle of Higher Education* reports, "almost a third of all full-time faculty members work at research universities with very high research activity," though it also claims that the "largest number of instructors teach at public, urban-serving, multi-campus institutions that grant associate degrees." As of 2011, there were approximately 170,000 tenure-track faculty at very high research activity universities, out of about 760,000 total full-time faculty.[37] This gives us a rough estimate that about 22% of full-time academic jobs involve significant levels of research.

Colleges today, as we saw above, have roughly a 34:16 tenure-track to non-tenure-track but full-time ratio. These ratios seem to be relatively stable over the past twenty years. So, given all this information, I offer some rough estimates. Of all the people who start a PhD program, about half will graduate.[38] About 12%–13% will get a tenure-track job, and another 6%–7% will get a non-tenure-track long-term job. Of the 20% or so people who get a long-term job, around 6% will get a (somewhat) research-focused tenure-track job, while the other 14% will get a teaching-focused long-term tenure-track or non-tenure-track job.

My friend and coauthor Chris Surprenant, a professor of philosophy and the director of the Honors Program at the University of New Orleans, warns readers to avoid what he calls the "Go Pro fallacy." This is the fallacy of concluding that if, say, 1 out of 10,000 Little League players eventually goes pro, then when *you* start Little League, you have a 1 in 10,000 chance of making the majors.[39]

You probably shouldn't interpret these raw percentages or ratios as your own odds or probabilities. Who makes it into pro baseball, and who finishes their PhD and gets a good job, is not random. Rather, most people who play Little League have, as I had, *zero* chance of making the majors, while some extraordinarily talented kids have a good chance.

A less dramatic version of that holds for graduate students. The people who follow my advice in the next few chapters have a decent chance of getting a long-term job; the ones who violate it have almost zero chance.[40]

How Much Do Professors Publish?

The thing that supposedly makes college professors distinct from, say, high school teachers, isn't just that professors have doctorates and teach older students. Rather, professors are generally trained to produce research for "peer-reviewed" journals and book outlets. ("Peer-reviewed" means that before something is published, it must be vetted, usually anonymously, by other experts in the field.) A high school teacher may teach chemistry or history, but he is not a chemist or a historian. A college professor who teaches chemistry or history is also supposed to be a chemist or a historian. A history teacher teaches history, but a historian *writes* history. A chemistry teacher conveys knowledge of chemistry; a chemist *creates* or discovers new chemistry knowledge.

With the exception of community college professors, all tenure-track faculty are expected to do *some* research. But how much do they actually do?

The Higher Education Research Institute (HERI) at UCLA conducts a biennial survey of professors' behaviors and attitudes at *four-year or greater* colleges and universities.

Survey results should be taken with a grain of salt. Anonymous survey respondents generally suffer from "social desirability bias": in surveys, people tend to exaggerate their good attributes and behaviors and understate their bad attributes and behaviors. For instance, people overstate how much they give to charity and understate how racist they are. For professors, since prestige is tied to publishing, this means that when surveyed, they probably exaggerate their number of publications. So, we should take the HERI numbers as an upper-bound—the truth is probably that faculty publish *less* than whatever the HERI survey reports.

The survey nevertheless indicates that a minority of faculty produce the majority of research. Twenty-eight percent of faculty at four-year or greater colleges say they have published *nothing* in the past two years, while another 31% say they've published only one or two pieces. About 60% of faculty average less than one publication a year. Another 20% published three or four pieces in the last two years, 14.7% published between five and ten pieces, 3.9% between eleven and twenty pieces, and 1.8% published twenty-one or more.[41]

The HERI data is not fine-grained enough to determine exactly what percentage of the faculty publishes what percentage of all research. But let's suppose that faculty tend to publish in the *middle* of the survey range. On that assumption, the top 20%—the most productive faculty—published two pieces for every single piece the bottom 80% published.[42]

These numbers may mislead you into thinking that professors publish more than they do. The HERI survey also asks professors how many *total* pieces they have published over their careers: 63.2% have never published a book, 44.9% have never published a chapter in an edited volume, and 17.2% have never published a single peer-reviewed article. Only about 21% have published twenty-one or more articles in their careers, while about 70% have published ten or fewer articles in their careers.[43]

This means that the minority of professors do most of the research. It suggests that 20% of faculty who have published at least twenty-one articles have, *at a bare minimum*, published as a group (over their careers) almost twice what the remaining 80% of faculty have collectively published over their entire careers.[44] That's probably a low estimate. Faculty at the high-end R1s publish many articles a year over their careers and tend to retire with many dozen or even hundreds of peer-reviewed articles published. What a professor publishes in a career at Southeast Nowhere State may be less than what the typical MIT professor publishes every two years.

Again, these numbers don't include community college and other two-year college faculty. This means the actual percentage of full-time faculty who regularly publish or conduct research is even lower. Keep in mind, also, that what counts as a good number of publications varies from field to field. Psychologists at low-ranked schools publish more than mathematicians at high-ranked schools.

To summarize, we looked at data surveying how much faculty publish, data classifying faculty by their status and the kind of college they work at, and data surveying faculty about how they spend their workweeks. All the data say the same thing: the overwhelming majority of full-time faculty, including full-time tenure-track faculty, spend most of their time on teaching-related activities. The overwhelming majority of full-time professors at four-year or greater colleges publish ten or fewer articles over their entire working lives.

What you should take from all this depends on what your goals are. At the very least, it's more information about how faculty spend their days. A minority do lots of research; most instead do lots of teaching. It also tells you that—assuming you're the representative average PhD student—the likelihood that you'll become a professor who publishes a great deal of research is low. Whether that's good or bad depends on your goals.

Researching the Small Things

Remember, only about a quarter of all full-time faculty get a research-focused job. Most faculty spend their days on teaching and service. Seventy percent of faculty at colleges that issue at least a BA degree publish ten or fewer articles in their entire career. A randomly selected first-year graduate student has about a one in twenty chance of ending up as a full-time academic researcher, but a ten in twenty chance of quitting before getting a PhD. In other words, a randomly selected first-year graduate student is ten times likelier to fail to get a PhD than to get a research-oriented job.

Still, tenure-track faculty must do *some* publishing to receive tenure or make full professor. In chapter 3, I discuss at greater length what it takes to do good research and publish consistently. Here, let's talk about what most research is really like.

Physical Review Letters is among the most prestigious peer-reviewed journals in academic physics. If you regularly publish in *PRL*, you're probably a well-paid superstar at a fancy university. Here are the "Editors' Suggested Titles" of the papers published in the December 2018 issue:

1   "First Evidence for the cos 2ß > 0 and Resolution of the Caribbo-Kobayashi-Maskawa Quark-Mixing Unitary Triangle Ambiguity."
2   "Predictive Simulations of Ionization Energies of Solvated Halide Ions with Relativistic Embedded Equation of Coupled Cluster Theory."
3   "Interface-Governed Deformation of Nanobubbles and Nanotents Formed by Two-Dimensional Materials."

The journal editors thought these papers were of greater/wider than normal interest and importance.

Here's the abstract (the published summary) of the second paper:

Molecular dynamics combined with relativistic electronic structure methods leads to a new benchmark for calculating solvation structures. A subsystem approach for obtaining electron binding energies in the valence region is presented and applied to the case of halide ions (X–, X = F–At) in water. This approach is based on electronic structure calculations combining the relativistic equation-of-motion coupled cluster method for electron detachment and density functional theory via the frozen density embedding approach, using structures from classical molecular dynamics with polarizable force fields for discrete systems (in our study, droplets containing the anion and 50 water molecules). Our results indicate that one can accurately capture both the large solvent effect observed for the halides and the splitting of their ionization signals due to the increasingly large spin-orbit coupling of the $p_{3/2}$–$p_{1/2}$ manifold across the series, at an affordable computational cost. Furthermore, owing to the quantum mechanical treatment of both solute and solvent electron binding energies of semiquantitative quality are also obtained for (bulk) water as by-products of the calculations for the halogens (in droplets).[45]

Got it? Note that the reason I posted this abstract, rather than the abstract of the first article, is that the first paper's abstract was even more obscure (to laypeople) and contained equations I'd have to rewrite in LaTeX.

I don't mean to disparage any of these works. They're impressive academic outputs, and their authors should be commended. Publishing in *Physical Review Letters* is no joke. Still, you might notice that these papers are on narrow, highly specialized topics. Most highly educated people, let alone most laypeople, wouldn't understand what these papers say, let alone whether what they say is significant.

That's how it goes. Most research is not "big," paradigm-shifting, ground-breaking stuff. The typical published academic paper is not "Look, we discovered a new element!" or "Here's a complete theory of interpersonal justice" or "Here's how to understand the symbolism of *One Hundred Years of Solitude*." Rather, it's more like, "Here's how this catalyst affects this chemical under these narrow conditions" or "Here's a significant flaw in the argument of footnote 538 of Rawls's *Theory of Justice*" or "Here's a likely unreplicable psychological experiment that finds that students who watch a scary movie before taking an ungraded math test in a laboratory are 3 percentage points likelier to cheat."

Most research papers are of little interest to anyone outside the author's narrow *sub*field. Indeed, most papers are of little interest even to the researchers working *inside* the narrow subfield or on that particular topic.

Contrary to what you may have heard, it's probably false that "half of all papers are never read by anyone other than the journal editors, referees, and the authors."[46] However, in the humanities, about 80% of papers are never cited by anyone else, while most papers in the social sciences, medicine, and the natural sciences are cited at least once.[47] These different outcomes may result partly from different citation practices. In the social sciences, natural sciences, and medicine, authors try to cite every published paper relevant to their work. (That doesn't mean they actually *read* those papers, though.) In the humanities, authors only cite papers they're actively engaging with. (This is one reason why comparing the citation count of an English professor to that of an economist or chemist is uninformative.)

In short, doing good research usually means studying a topic so narrow that you can do extremely rigorous work but also so narrow that most people, including other experts, don't and won't care in the slightest what you have to say.

Academic researchers have tremendous freedom. No one tells you what to research. You're free to research anything you please, and you can publish at any venue where you can pass peer review. Some people use this freedom to revolutionize our understanding of justice, gravity, or rationality. Some use it to determine the twentieth digit of a constant in someone else's equation. And some use it to mourn their dead cats.

For many professors, the pressure to publish is so severe—or the rewards of publishing so high—that in recent years a number of "bullshit," or fake, academic journals with low standards have appeared. I literally receive at least one invitation a working day to publish in or join the "board" of some new "journal" published by a no-name company in the middle of nowhere. These "journals" often have zero standards, but instead require faculty to pay to publish. They have names similar to those of legitimate journals. The business model seems to be that some faculty could "publish" at these journals and then trick deans into thinking these are legitimate publications.

What Are the Students Like? What Is It Like to Teach?

Most full-time faculty spend most of their time teaching undergraduates; only a minority of faculty spend significant time doing research or teaching graduate students. So, to determine whether a professor job is for you, you need to know whether you'd like teaching.

As of 2015–16, the average combined mathematics and critical reading SAT score of all high school students taking the

SAT was 990, according to the US Department of Education.[48] In 2018, the College Board (which creates and administers the SAT) claimed the mean score was 1068.[49] Because of college selectivity, the average SAT score for students who actually enroll in college should be higher than that, while the average of students who actually finish college is probably higher still. College students are probably smarter on average than the population at large.

Still, these averages tell you little. There is tremendous variation in what students are like and in what it's like to teach them. Teaching undergraduates at Harvard is not the same as teaching students at Boston College, the University of Massachusetts at Amherst, the University of Massachusetts at Boston, or Bunker Hill Community College.

At some colleges, students are hardworking and studious. At others, they try to minimize coursework and maximize extracurricular fun. At some colleges, students are well-prepared for work at the college level. At others, they don't seem to be prepared to do even middle-school-level work. At some colleges, you would predominantly teach students who have a genuine curiosity about your field and class. At others, your students would mainly be conscripts taking your courses to satisfy general education requirements. At some colleges, most students care only about grades and credentials; at others, they care about learning for learning's sake. At some colleges, students are intellectuals; at others, philistines. At some colleges, students will do all the reading and understand it. At some, they'll do the reading but won't understand it. At others, they won't do the reading. At some colleges, faculty are expected to work hard to make students happy, to keep enrollments up, to tutor students and ensure that students pass the classes, and even to act in loco parentis and watch out for students' welfare. At other colleges, faculty have no such obligations.

Insert "in general" in front of every sentence in the last paragraph. While the typical student varies from school to school, there's also tremendous variation among the students within any individual school. For instance, I received my PhD in philosophy at the University of Arizona, a large flagship state university with the top-ranked graduate program in political philosophy. As a teaching assistant, I led discussion sections of introductory general education classes. Most of my students at the 101-level couldn't write a coherent argumentative essay. My ninth-grade honors English class in the middle of nowhere, New Hampshire, had better writers with higher reading comprehension. Nevertheless, senior philosophy majors at Arizona were on par with the senior philosophy majors I met at Brown, where I got my first job.

In 2011, Richard Arum and Josipa Roksa published *Academically Adrift: Limited Learning on College Campuses*. It paints a grim picture of what students do—and don't do. The short summary is that most students put little time and effort into learning. Most students also learn little to nothing in college. The small minority who demonstrate measurable gains also tend to be the small minority who put in significant effort.

Arum and Roksa claim that in 1960, the average college student spent about forty hours a week focused on academic activities, such as attending classes, doing homework, or studying. Today, the average student in the University of California system spends roughly three hours of leisure for each hour studying.[50] The average college student now treats academic work as a part-time, roughly twenty-seven-hour-a-week job.

To test for learning, Arum and Roksa administered the Collegiate Learning Assessment (CLA) exam to students at various colleges over a multiple-year period, trying to see if students showed improvement as they studied. Their results are depressing. The average student who took the test in the fall of 2005 showed only a seven percentile point improvement in complex reasoning, critical thinking, and writing skills by the end of her sophomore year. The measured gains, they note, were negligible.[51] They say that "at least 45 percent of students in our sample did not demonstrate any statistically significant improvement in CLA performance during the first two years of college."[52] At least 36% walked away with no measured gains after four years of college. More conservative and cautious approaches to testing statistical significance yield worse results: at least 53% had no gains after two years.[53] Worse, the majority of students who did improve their CLA scores generally had only *modest* gains. Only about one-tenth of students demonstrated large gains.

So, in deciding whether you want to be a professor, ask: Am I willing to spend the majority of my working life teaching mostly mediocre undergraduates, knowing that for the vast majority, my class will impart no increase in their reasoning or writing skills? You might end up with a better teaching situation than that, but that's the typical deal.

Is Academia for You?

Academia is good work, if you can get it. Even the "bad" academic jobs are pretty great, compared to most other jobs out there. Various surveys find that college professors have high rates of job satisfaction.[54]

By now, you've got a snapshot idea of what academic life is like. You know about the distribution and diversity of job experiences. You have a rough sense of the "odds" of getting any kind of permanent/long-term academic job. You have a sense of what the typical or average jobs look like. Should you go to graduate school and pursue an academic career?

My mentor, the philosopher and economist David Schmidtz, advises his students to ask themselves, "What's the lowest pay, lowest status, lowest-perks job I'd be happy with?" Go ahead and ask yourself that.

If your answer is, "I'd be okay with high-paying, research-intensive, freedom-filled tenure-track positions at any of the Ivy League Schools, their peers, or Berkeley and Michigan," then you probably shouldn't go. You probably won't get such a job.

If your answer is, "I'd be happy to spend most of my time teaching mostly disinterested undergrads with an average SAT score of 1100, as a tenure-track professor at a mid-ranked college for $68K/year," then maybe you should go to grad school. Even then, I say "maybe." The chances that a randomly selected first-year PhD student will get even a job like this are low, indeed, less than 50%. (After all, 50% never complete their degree.)

I'm not saying the Ivy League job is in fact better than the average job, but I am saying that if you can only be happy with the highest paying and highest status jobs, entering academia is a risky proposition. You may be the smartest, most talented, most driven psychology major your college has seen in twenty years. Still, when and if you hit the psychology professor job market, you'll be competing against one thousand other "best psych majors in twenty years" from around the world. (I talk more about the job market in chapter 4.)

If you would be happy with the typical faculty gig, then I recommend you keep reading. Over the next few chapters, I'll offer the best advice I can about being productive in graduate school, managing a work/life balance, avoiding stress and burnout, and maximizing your chances of getting the gig you want. My advice doesn't guarantee good results, but failing to heed it all but guarantees bad results.

UPSHOTS

- You should know what it's like to be a professor before you worry about how to succeed.
- Most professors spend most of their time teaching and doing service work; only a minority spends significant amounts of time doing research.
- Pay, prestige, and job flexibility are tied to research more than teaching.
- There are tenure-track, long-term non-tenure-track, and temporary jobs.
- Adjuncts make up 50% of the faculty work force, but they are not replacing full-time professors. The ratio of full-time professors to students has remained constant over fifty years.
- Professors make the most money at research-intensive universities. Pay varies tremendously across disciplines, university type, and so on. At doctoral universities, the 95th percentile of professors makes more than $200,000 in salary; at four-year-only colleges, the 10th percentile of professors makes under $50,000.
- Of all the people who start a PhD, roughly half will graduate. Roughly one-fifth will get a full-time faculty job. Slightly more than one-tenth will get a tenure-track job. Around one-twentieth will get a tenure-track job at a research-intensive school.
- These percentages are not odds. Your chances depend on your field, your department's rank, and *you*. Some PhD students have no chance of getting a long-term job; some have a close to 100% chance.
- Of full-time professors at four-year or greater colleges, 70% have published ten or fewer pieces in their careers.
- Most research is on relatively narrow and specialized topics, of little interest to most people in the field. Most research has a low impact.
- Undergraduates vary tremendously in terms of talent and motivation.
- If you'd be happy only as a tenure-track professor at an Ivy League school or the equivalent, going into academia is a bad idea. The chances of landing any job, let alone that kind of job, are too low.

TWO

Success in Graduate School Means Working to Get a Job

The Olympics Analogy

If you want to become a professor, you should spend your time in graduate school doing what it takes to become competitive in the academic job market. A faculty job is the nail for which a PhD is a hammer. A faculty job is the destination for which a PhD is the road. While some STEM and economics PhDs enjoy many good opportunities outside academia, many humanities and social science PhDs' strongest job prospects are in the academy.

As a graduate student, you are training for the Olympics. You are trying to win a faculty job. You will be competing against three hundred to one thousand people who are the best in the world at what you study. Your least qualified competitors will be impressive people with decent credentials. Your best qualified competitors spend all five (or more) years of graduate school teaching innovative classes, publishing papers in top peer-reviewed journals, networking with people around the world, and amassing a résumé on a par with or better than the résumé of most currently employed assistant professors.

They spend their entire grad school career training to get the job you want. If you want a job, you must not only *be* better than they are, but *look better* on paper. You must amass a résumé that makes it obvious how good you are.

The philosopher and economist David Schmidtz offers the following analogy to his students: Imagine you meet someone who says she intends to win gold at the Olympics four years from now. You ask her what her training regimen looks like. She responds, "I'm not training yet. The Olympics are years away. I'll start training when the time comes. I expect the Olympic committee to exercise due diligence and find the best raw talent. It's not my job to do their job for them, to help them select the best people. I work best under pressure anyway."

This person is destined to fail. She doesn't understand the Olympics or what it takes to compete. Dave adds that in the academic job market, there is no silver medal. For any job search, being the second-choice candidate plus $2 will buy you a cup of coffee. The good news is that all it takes is one gold medal—one job offer—to have a happy, fulfilling life-long career.

My main advice is simple: If you want an academic job, you must treat graduate school as *professional school*. You must hit the ground running if you want to get anywhere.

Remember, I'm not endorsing the way things are. Maybe it's regrettable that students have to professionalize so much and so soon. Maybe this reflects the perverse influence of neoliberalism or an unjustifiable arms race over scarce opportunities. Maybe not. Regardless, this book is about succeeding in academia as it is, not about how to succeed in academia as it should be.

In this chapter, I'll discuss what grad school is like and offer advice specifically for navigating it. In the next chapter, I discuss at great length how to manage your time, produce high levels of research, and so on. That advice applies to faculty with steady jobs, but it's *especially* important for graduate students if they ever want to get a job.

I'm Not Your Best Friend. I'm Your Only Friend

Some graduate students dislike the kind of advice I'm about to give. When I've given talks on these issues, some students protest that the point of grad school is to read, learn, grow, and cultivate their intellects. They say the emphasis on professionalization and job market strategy sucks the vigor out of their education. Graduate school should be an escape from the rat race, not the start of the rat race. Getting a PhD shouldn't feel like getting an MBA.

I understand where they're coming from. Still, this kind of objection presumes a false dichotomy. It also misunderstands the way graduate school is supposed to help you grow. Professionalizing in grad school primarily means *publishing*. It's not as if the students who use their time to learn how to write and publish articles in A-level journals generally fail to cultivate their intellects, while the students who just read all day and never produce anything in turn grow the most. It's not as if grad students who spend their days researching in the lab grow less than the students who just read and think.

On the contrary, the latter kinds of student practice being students, and students they remain.

The point of the PhD is to make you into a professor, and you don't become a professor by perfecting the art of being a student. The students who professionalize early are also the students who transform themselves from students into researchers/teachers/colleagues. You succeed in grad school when you turn yourself into a professional.

You Have Twenty Seconds

The last time we held a tenure-track assistant professor search within my subfield in my academic department, we received five hundred applications. The search committee first whittled that down to about seventy applicants whom we looked at more closely. We then cut that to twelve, whom we interviewed over the phone, and finally to five, whom we brought to campus for a full interview.

An academic job application can be more than one hundred pages long. It includes the applicant's CV (curriculum vitae, the academic version of a résumé), four to six recommendation letters, a few writing samples, evidence of teaching effectiveness, a description of the applicant's research goals, statements about his teaching philosophy, sample syllabi, and so on.

One hundred pages. Still, the modal amount of time we spend looking at individual applications in the first round was about twenty seconds. Most of us skip cover letters and go straight to candidates' CVs. First question: Where did the candidate get her PhD? Second question: Does the job candidate have a large number of published papers in prestigious journals? Candidates from good schools with many publications went into the "further scrutiny" pile. The other 430 went into the reject pile after a twenty-second skim.

Maybe the best candidate—the one who would have performed the best—went in the reject pile after that twenty-second skim. So it goes. We're not going to go looking for the hidden diamond in the rough when we have a pile of diamonds in front of us. We have neither the time nor the ability to discover the hidden geniuses with latent talent.

When I talk to my colleagues at other universities, I get similar stories. Some generous faculty give you a full minute to make the first cut. But no one is spending much more time than that.

One minute (or less) per application in the first pass? That's by necessity. If my colleagues and I each spent, say, one hour per application, we'd then each dedicate five hundred hours—one-quarter of our working year—just to the first round of applications. No university wants its faculty to do that. (At Georgetown, as a full professor, "service to the university, profession, and community" officially counts for only 15% of the job.) No one has the time for it.

I once was chatting with a grad student from Oxford. He said he had no intention of publishing, giving talks, or doing other things to build up his CV. He said, "I expect hiring committees to *discover* me." Maybe that works for Oxford graduates seeking jobs in the United Kingdom. It doesn't work in the United States. In the US, it's your job to craft an outstanding CV. Hiring committees don't regard it as their job to descry your invisible brilliance.

How to Get into Graduate School

The first step to becoming a professor is to go to graduate school and get a PhD. At most four-year colleges, full-time faculty must possess a PhD or equivalent terminal degree. In the past, you might be offered a long-term, non-tenure-track instructor slot with only a master's. Today, there's a glut of PhDs; in most fields, the ratio of newly minted PhDs to entry-level jobs keeps increasing. There's a backlog of PhDs who failed to get jobs in the previous year, who keep competing for the new jobs against the new PhDs. You have zero chance of getting a tenure-track job and almost zero chance of getting a non-tenure-track job without a PhD.

There are many books about how to do well in graduate school admissions. I'd recommend perusing a few. But the truth is, there's not much magic to it. You need to write a nice statement of purpose, one that demonstrates your passion for the field, that explains why you want to work in academia, that shows not only that you have a few original ideas but also that you are open-minded and eager to learn from the professors at the departments to which you apply. You must have a high-quality, original writing sample that shows you can do high-level academic work. As much as possible, the writing sample should read less like an undergraduate essay and more like an original *article* an assistant professor would write and publish. You must have good grades in your field and outstanding, over-the-top flattering letters of recommendation from your undergrad professors, each of which states you're the best (fill in the blank) major in twenty years. You'll also want high Graduate Record Exam scores, though some universities are now waiving the GRE requirement.

A number of websites publish the average GRE scores of different majors. I won't insert a table here, because you can google these with ease. Let me instead explain what the numbers mean for you.

Philosophy majors who take the GRE average 160 verbal (out of 170), 154 quantitative (out of 170), and 4.3 (out of 6) in analytical writing.[1] Remember that these are the averages of all the philosophy students who take the GRE. Generally, the students who succeed in getting into graduate school, especially the highly ranked programs, have significantly higher scores than that. Some schools weight GREs more than others, but the general rule is that you should have scores significantly above the average in your undergraduate major. That's tough, because the people who take the GRE are already above average. Thus, the numbers you see online for your field are not the numbers to match. They're numbers to beat.

Ideally, as an undergraduate hoping for admission to a good graduate program, you went to a name brand college or university, such as an Ivy League research university or one of its peers. As economist Joni Hersch summarizes her research in this area:

> Income disparities arise not only from differences in the level of education but also from differences in status associated with an individual's degree-granting college or university. While higher ability among those who graduate from elite undergraduate institutions may account for much of the earnings premium associated with elite education, ability should be largely equalized among those who graduate from similarly selective graduate programs. Few graduates of nonselective institutions earn post-baccalaureate degrees from elite institutions, and even when they do, undergraduate institutional prestige continues to influence earnings overall and among those with law, medical, graduate business and doctoral degrees.[2]

Hersch finds that even graduates of the elite liberal arts colleges are at a significant disadvantage in getting admission into the top-ranked academic programs. Prospects for people who go to run-of-the-mill colleges are lower still. Their future earnings and future career prospects—regardless of whether they pursue a PhD, a JD, an MD, an MBA, or some other graduate degree—are lower.

I'm not saying this is fair or unfair. Maybe this reflects "prestige bias." Maybe not: maybe so-called prestige bias isn't a bias. Maybe undergraduates from the elite research schools are indeed the best trained, because they studied with the kinds of professors who also teach graduate level work and produce the most research. For your purposes, it doesn't matter what the reason is and whether it's fair or not. What matters to you is that in general, the student from Harvard will have a better chance of getting into the better PhD programs than an otherwise identical student from UConn or Trinity College.

The good news is that once you're in grad school, your undergrad degree won't matter as much. People will instead judge you largely by the rank and reputation of your graduate program. The bad news is that they will judge you largely by the rank and reputation of your graduate program. That brings me to the next point.

Go to the Highest-Ranked Graduate School You Can

Academia is a prestige economy. That's especially true for getting a job. The prestige of your graduate program and of your advisor greatly determine your job prospects.

Universities and colleges are divided into various fields, housed in autonomous academic departments, such as physics, finance, comparative literature, political science, economics, or whatnot. Academic departments usually operate independently of other departments at the same university. They have their own standards of excellence and often conduct their hiring without consulting people from any other department. As a graduate student or faculty member, you rarely interact with members of other academic departments. (I've worked at Georgetown for almost eight years, but I know the names of only six buildings.)

In any given academic field, somewhere between fifty to two hundred American universities offer a PhD. PhD programs are not created equal. Some PhD programs have the most productive and innovative research faculty in the world.

Some have faculty who barely and rarely publish. Some have faculty who care deeply about their students and endeavor to help them succeed. Some have faculty who hate each other and who are indifferent to their students. Some have faculty who routinely sexually harass their students or who expect students to kiss their asses.[3] Some faculty treat their students as respected apprentices, while others exploit them for cheap labor. Some faculty insist that grad students call them by their first names, while other faculty insist their grad students address them as Professor or Doctor such-and-such.

When selecting graduate schools, you should try to enter programs with a strong reputation for being supportive and nurturing. To determine what the departmental atmosphere is like, you can email current PhD students in those departments. Most departments maintain a public list of their graduate students on their websites. You can also scour the internet for rumors about departmental reputations, though these websites are often disreputable themselves. Be wary of professors who will exploit you once you depend on them.

Your graduate department's *rank* or *reputation* determines your basic job prospects. Various academic journals, news magazines (such as *US News and World Report*), and websites create and maintain these rankings. Study them carefully. The rankings for specific graduate programs don't necessarily correspond to the overall ranking of the school or its undergraduate program. An Ivy League school might have a lousy graduate program in X, while East Nowhere State's PhD in Y could be the best in the world.

For instance, in philosophy, as of 2017–18, here are the top twelve PhD programs:

1 New York University
2 Rutgers (New Brunswick), Princeton

4 Michigan (Ann Arbor)
5 Yale
6 Harvard, Pittsburgh
8 Stanford, University of Southern California
10 Columbia, Berkeley, UCLA

You might be surprised to see that NYU and Rutgers are the top two. Indeed, they've both consistently outranked the Ivies for twenty years or more. The University of Pittsburgh has been a philosophy powerhouse forever. Go figure.

It's also important to examine how volatile an individual department is. Ideally, you'd want to enroll in a department that is stable or moving up. You don't want to get stuck at a program that might collapse while you're there. Your advisors might move on to greener pastures but leave you behind.

In general, the PhD students who attend top-ranked graduate programs will have a much easier time getting *any* long-term academic job than the people who attend lower-ranked or unranked programs. They'll also have an easier time getting the more lucrative and higher prestige jobs.

Take a close look at the departmental websites of any program to which you're considering applying. Many maintain tables documenting how many PhD students they've graduated, what their subfields were, whether they got job offers and what kind of job offers they received upon graduation, and what their current jobs are.

If you see that a program hasn't placed a single person in a tenure-track job in twenty years, then they almost certainly won't place *you* in a tenure-track job. If you see that they regularly place people in teaching but not research jobs, then you'll probably get a teaching job. The kinds of jobs students have been getting in the past five years are the kinds of jobs you can expect to get. If they place 50% of their graduates in an academic job, then you have about a 50% chance of getting an academic job. (Adjust the percentages based upon your individual CV.)

You should also learn what the recent graduates who got jobs were like—and copy their behavior. They tend to be the better students, though placement also depends on subfields. Grad student Mike might be the best overall student, but maybe no one wanted to hire someone—even the best new person—specializing in medieval Dutch history. If you find that students who specialize in X get jobs but students who specialize in Y don't, that's instructive.

Copying the recently successful grad students isn't good enough. The job market keeps getting more difficult. The number of people applying for jobs continues to grow faster than the number of jobs. (I'll give you some numbers in chapter 4.) As a result, it's a buyer's market. At some universities, the number of publications it took to earn *tenure* twenty years ago is what it takes to get the *job* today. What it took for me to get my first job is probably less than what it would take for you to get the equivalent job now or ten years from now. So, the real advice is to find the most successful people in your program, and then make yourself even more impressive.

You'll probably notice that only the top ten or so programs in any field regularly place their graduates in the higher-paying, higher-status research-focused jobs. Even then, sometimes the highest-ranked programs struggle, especially with certain subfields. For instance, in the political science subfield of political theory, there might be only twenty tenure-track jobs in a given year, while the top ten departments will by themselves put out maybe twice that many candidates.

I claimed that the prestige of one's graduate program (and the general prestige of that university) has a massive influence over one's chances of getting any academic job. To illustrate, let's examine English. In a 2015 study, economists David Colander and Daisy Zhuo tracked English PhD job placements from 2008 to 2011. They concluded that graduating from one of the top six English programs improves both the type of position a candidate is able to secure and the ranking of the hiring institution. About 70% of graduates from the top six departments secure either a tenure-track job or a prestigious postdoc upon graduation, with about one-third getting a research-oriented tenure-track job at graduation. While over 40% of the students from the "tier 4" graduate programs (ranked 63rd or lower) managed to get tenure-track jobs, those jobs tended to be at lower-ranked colleges and universities, with higher teaching loads and less pay. The top three *tiers* of programs—that is, the top sixty-two English programs at research universities—almost always hire graduates from the top six individual programs.[4] In short, the top six programs dominate the field when it comes to hiring.

If you want to succeed in academia, go to the best graduate program with the best job placement you can. This trumps almost everything else, including fit, whether you share the same research interests as the faculty there, the size of the graduate stipend, or the location of the university.

How Long Does Graduate School Last? What Happens There?

Nominally, most PhD programs in the United States are designed to last five years. Some fields might aim at four or six years instead.

That's the nominal time-to-PhD. In fact, the typical PhD student doesn't graduate "on time." CBS News reports the *mean* time to graduate to be 8.2 years.[5] The *Chronicle of Higher Education* estimates instead that the *median* time to graduate is 7.5 years, with a median of 11.7 years in education, 9.2 in the humanities, 7.7 years in the social sciences, and just under 7 years in engineering, the life sciences, and the physical sciences.[6]

You really should try to finish on time. Many graduate programs only guarantee graduate living stipends for five years. After that, you might be stuck teaching as an adjunct for very low pay while you struggle to finish your PhD.

The normal progression toward the PhD goes something like this:

1   For the first three years, you take graduate-level seminars and classes, usually three or four classes a semester. You'll probably have to complete some general-education-style distribution of courses within your field. In some programs, that might mean everyone takes the same classes for two years. In others, it means that you must take, say, two courses from four different areas, or subfields. You'll also get to take a few classes specifically within the subfield in which you plan to specialize.

2   Around year 3, you'll sit for what are called *preliminary*, *qualifying*, or *comprehensive* (comp) exams. Often this means selecting two to three subfields in your discipline. You read a large number of both classic and cutting-edge books and papers in those fields. You then take a three- to four-hour written exam in each subfield you selected. If your written exams are good enough, you then sit for a three-hour oral exam, in which the graduate faculty grill you with tough questions and criticize your written exam answers at length. If you pass this exam, you continue to step three. If you fail, you are permitted a second chance to pass the comps in six months, or you might simply fail

out of the program. By the way, studying for comp exams occurs independently of other classes you are taking. Upon completing the comp exams, you may automatically earn a master's degree in your field. But you're not finished yet.

3 After you pass your comp exams, you then form a dissertation committee and select a dissertation advisor/ supervisor. You then write a prospectus—a long proposal and outline of what you intend to write for your dissertation, perhaps along with a sample chapter. You submit the prospectus to the committee. If it's good enough on paper, you'll get to sit for an oral prospectus exam. The purpose of this exam is for faculty to critique your proposal, offer you advice, and help ensure that your idea for your dissertation is worth pursuing. They want to sign off on your idea before they set you free to spend two to five years working on original research. If you pass, you are considered ABD—All But Dissertation—and you move on to the final step. If you fail the written or oral portion of the prospectus exam, you might be granted another six months to attempt to produce a new prospectus on a new research topic. If you fail twice, you'll be kicked out of the program, usually with a master's degree as a consolation prize. Many students fail out of their program at this stage.[7]

4 You then write your dissertation. A dissertation might be the equivalent of three to five closely related but independent papers. It might instead be a three-hundred-page book on some subject. In mathematics, it may be as short as fifty pages. In history, it may be five hundred pages. Once your dissertation is finished, you submit it to your advisory committee. Usually they will have already read parts of it and told you how to improve it before you officially submit it. If they think the

written work is good enough, they will let you sit for the defense. At many schools, faculty won't let you officially submit the dissertation for a defense unless they are confident you can pass, but this isn't a universal practice. It's certainly possible to fail a defense. During the defense, your committee grills you and critiques your work for three hours, asking you hard questions, trying to poke holes in your model, your arguments, your data, and so on. If you fail, you fail the program and leave with a master's degree as a consolation prize. If you succeed, they shake your hand, break out the champagne, and say, "Congratulations, Dr. _____." You're now a PhD!

Remember: Getting a PhD is a necessary step for getting an academic job. Nevertheless, on average, only about two out of five new PhDs will get a long-term faculty job. In some fields, the numbers are better; in others, worse.

How Much Does a PhD Cost?

A PhD is free—sort of. In fact, you get paid to study for it. Good PhD programs waive students' tuition. Every PhD student in good standing gets a full-ride academic scholarship.

Good PhD programs also provide students with a living stipend, usually between $15,000 and $30,000, guaranteed for five or six years. The size of the stipend depends upon the school's/department's resources and the local cost of living. In some fields, it depends upon your advisor—who might be paying you a stipend out of an NSF grant. This stipend won't make you rich, but with that much money, you can probably at least live better than you did as an undergraduate. The stipend is sometimes given as an unconditional fellowship, but it often requires students to work as graduate teaching assistants or as research assistants in a laboratory.

You should not pay to get a PhD. (The exception: You are getting a PhD in engineering or one of the rare disciplines that easily leads to $200,000+/year jobs in industry.) Repeat: Do not pay for a PhD. Do not take on debt to get a PhD. Do not pay any tuition for your PhD.

Let's say you apply to a number of graduate schools. You earn a few offers of admission. None of the PhD programs offers to waive tuition and none offers you a living stipend. That's a sign of one of two things: (1) the graduate program is bad and is unlikely to help you get an academic job; or (2) the program might be good, but they don't see *you* as good.

If no program offers you a full ride with a living stipend, that's a strong signal that your chances of succeeding in academia are negligible. No doubt there are some rock-star professors out there who paid their own way. But these are the rules: Never take on debt to get a PhD; don't attend a program unless they give you a full ride and a living stipend. A good graduate program treats you like a paid apprentice. A bad graduate program treats you like a tuition-paying student.

If you only receive offers that require you to pay tuition or that fail to offer you a living stipend, you should decline, even if that means giving up on academia. You might try applying again a year later, perhaps after improving your writing sample or retaking the GRE. You might instead apply to a terminal master's program in your field. Some high-quality master's programs offer living stipends and full rides to their students. You can use your new and better credentials to then try to obtain a full ride at a better PhD program. But whatever you do, don't take on debt and don't pay for your PhD.

Nevertheless, even though this is universal advice, around 40% of grad students end up borrowing money to finish their

PhD. On average, they accrue $37,000 in debt.[8] I can't find data on who these students are. I suspect, however, that these are mostly (a) students going to the weak programs, and (b) students at stronger programs who took too long to finish and thus outlasted their five to six years of guaranteed living stipends.

I said graduate school is "sort of" free. Even though they pay you to go, you still give up something to be there. While you're spending the median seven and a half years in grad school, you could instead have worked at a high-paying full-time job. If a grad student isn't careful and strategic, it's easy for him to enter his mid-thirties with no savings, living in a crummy apartment, eating cheap noodles and cereal for dinner, with no car, no family, and few prospects. Meanwhile, his friends from college have achieved career success, bought a house, amassed significant retirement savings, and started their families.

Graduate school has a high opportunity cost. The longer you take, the higher the cost, even if you don't pay a dollar of tuition, and even if you get a living stipend.

Graduate School Is Relatively Easy

PhD students often feel overwhelmed and anxious. Compared to faculty, they suffer from high rates of mental health problems.[9] Graduate students often feel like imposters.[10] It often feels as if all the other students are smarter, more creative, and more productive.

Part of the problem is that PhD students were usually excellent undergraduate students, but graduate school is not an extension of undergraduate education. Undergrads train to understand and sometimes apply previously generated knowledge. Graduate students are training to become knowledge creators. (As we saw in chapter 1, most of them will become teachers, not researchers, but graduate school nevertheless trains students to do research.) They must learn to think like researchers, not like undergraduates. This means not merely understanding material, but learning to find holes and problems in leading researchers' work. It also means being able to synthesize ideas and craft new research projects.

At the same time, graduate students must balance different forms of work. They must read hundreds of pages of material per week, write short and long papers, and prepare for exams. In exchange for their living stipends, many must work in laboratories or as teaching assistants. Often students have poor time-management skills.

Graduate school is a full-time job. In a way, it's quite hard. No wonder half the students fail or quit. All that said, graduate school is—in terms of responsibility—the easiest time you'll have in your entire academic career. Things get harder once you become a professor. Consider: In graduate school, your professors are often doing cutting-edge research and are the most expert people in the entire world on certain topics. They'll tell you what you need to read and know to be at the forefront. They tell you what would count as "making a move" in the field. They issue-spot for you and coach you on how to write papers that advance the conversation on that topic.

When you become a professor, that mentoring disappears. No one gets paid to feed you research ideas anymore. You no longer have six experts helping you write publishable papers each year. You have to do all that work on your own.

In graduate school, you may be asked to work twenty hours per week as a graduate TA in one class per semester. As you'll see below, if you manage your time properly, this really means working five or six hours on most weeks, some of which can be simultaneously used for reading or writing. The professor you serve will design the class, write the syllabus, and assign the readings.

As a faculty member, you'll most likely teach between three and five classes a semester. You now have to write your own syllabi, tests, and assignments, and determine how classes will go. You're now in charge, and you must do far more teaching work. You may have to grade hundreds of papers or exams every few weeks. Even professors with light teaching loads at research-intensive universities spend far more time teaching than grad students do. However much teaching you do in grad school, you'll do more as a professor.

As a grad student, you must read a great deal to learn a field. As a professor, you've already got that reading under your belt. But you must still keep abreast of changes and developments in the field. You'll still read dozens of books and hundreds of papers per year. You must keep up with the field so you don't get left behind. Reading doesn't go away. As a professor, no one tells you what you need to read to keep up.

As a grad student, you have no service expectations. You don't serve on admissions, gen-ed, hiring, or other regular or ad hoc committees. You don't have to referee papers for peer-reviewed journals. You don't march in graduation ceremonies or help hire new faculty. Newly minted assistant professors do all this and more. More senior faculty have it worse. As the surveys we discussed in chapter 1 show, the average college professor outside of the R1s spends around ten hours a week on various forms of service.

As a student, you aren't required to publish. You certainly *should* publish (see chapter 4), but publishing isn't a requirement for you to graduate with a 4.0 GPA and glowing letters of recommendation. As an assistant professor, you must publish at least a few papers in decent journals, or you will be fired. If you receive a research job, you may have to publish six to ten papers (or more, depending on the field), plus a book, all with the top publishers, with acceptance rates below 5%. You'll have to ensure that these papers are widely read and influential. Otherwise, you'll be fired after six years of probation.

Consider also that your home life is likely to be more difficult as a professor than as a graduate student. For instance, you're more likely to have kids—if you ever have them—as a young assistant professor than as a grad student. Try teaching six classes a year, doing ten-plus hours of service a week, and conducting original research, all while getting no sleep because your infant has colic.

This brings me to some stark advice. If you find that you hate grad school, if you find everything you do to be a massive struggle, you should first read the rest of this book to ensure you're not suffering from a time-management/strategy problem. But if you take my advice about time management and nevertheless still hate grad school, you should consider quitting. It doesn't get easier. You will never have less expected of you and never face less pressure than you will as a graduate student.

How to Make Your Time as Teaching Assistant Work for You

In the humanities, social sciences, and even in the natural sciences, graduate students usually receive their living stipends in exchange for working as teaching assistants, often for large 101-type introductory/gen-ed courses with hundreds of disinterested undergrads. As a teaching assistant, you may be required to attend your professor's main lectures for two classes a week, then lead two to three smaller discussion sections on Fridays. You'll be expected to grade all the papers and tests for the fifty to ninety students in your sections. You'll hold two to three office hours per week, which means you'll sit in the TA office, ready to tutor or talk to any students who decide to drop in.

As a teaching assistant, your university may say on paper that you're expected to work twenty hours a week. You aren't really. Don't. They say twenty hours for political reasons, to appease state legislators or the board of trustees. In reality, you should work about five hours a week on the typical week and maybe ten on weeks you have to grade papers and exams. If you spend more than that, you're doing it wrong and sabotaging your career.

This isn't an economics book, but here's a relevant economics lesson. In classical economics, the now discredited labor theory of value held that the value of a final product or service is determined by the amount of labor that goes into that product or service. Since the 1870s, we've known that the labor theory of value is false. The value of the final product is instead determined by the forces of supply and demand, and the value of the labor that goes into the final product is itself largely determined by the value of the final product. The labor theory of value is not just false but backward. More labor doesn't mean something is worth more.

Many students seem nevertheless to believe that the labor theory of value applies to teaching: the more time I spend preparing, the better a teacher I must be. Nope. You need to disabuse yourself of this myth. Good teachers rock their classes but also ensure that teaching doesn't swallow all their time.

Suppose it takes you twenty hours a week to prepare discussion sections of someone else's class. With that kind of work routine, you're not going to hack it as a professor, when you'll instead have two to five distinct courses of your own to teach a week. If it takes you this long to prepare, you're either wasting your time—putting in effort far past the point of diminishing returns—or *you're bad at teaching*. This isn't the job for you.

As a TA, you might have to attend your professor's main lectures for two hours a week. During those hours, don't sit back and congratulate yourself that you already know the material. Instead, use that time productively. While your professor lectures, prepare anything you'll need for your discussion sections, such as handouts, slides, games, or activities. You should think like a teacher, and determine how you would present and explain that very same material. You should grade papers and quizzes. You should take the time to design your own syllabus. If you're a TA for Government 101, you should walk out of the semester with your own version of Government 101 prepared and ready to go.

If you have to serve as a TA ten times in ten distinct classes, then by the time you graduate, you should have ten or so classes prepped. If you later get a faculty job, you'll have less prep, because you already have those ten classes ready to go.

If your professor has a problem with you doing prep work while he lectures, then your professor is a jerk who is sabotaging your future. Slip a copy of this page (where I call him a jerk) under his office door.

During your office hours, don't sit around twiddling your thumbs. Write. Do your class work. Read for your classes or comp exams. If you have to grade, grade. Bring your laptop—and a pair of noise-canceling earphones if you're sharing the office—and write your seminar papers or dissertation. When a student comes in for help, stop and help, and then get back to doing your real work. Holding office hours means you must help any students who show up, but it doesn't mean you're forbidden from doing your own work when no one's there.

There are plenty of ways to reduce preparation time for classes. For one, you shouldn't write out an entire lecture. Your PowerPoint slides, if you use those, should probably have less text. Your fellow grad students and professors might be willing to share their teaching materials. (I, for one, make it a point to offer all of my slides and teaching materials to my colleagues and any of our postdocs. Heck, I'll give them to strangers, including you.) You can try inverting the classroom: each week, assign two or three undergraduate students to be discussion leaders who must present the material and lead discussion among their peers. You can give undergrads a list of questions to discuss ahead of time and have them come in with pre-written answers, ready to talk. At any rate, you should be able to teach a 101-style class off the cuff.

I return to this point in chapter 3, but I'll introduce it here: Don't dwell on teaching. Even though most faculty become full-time teachers rather than researchers, don't dwell on teaching. If you want to get a job, even a full-time teaching job, publishing beats teaching. Plus, only the people who finish get jobs. The grad students who spend the most time "perfecting their teaching" often fail out of their programs and thus never get careers as teachers. It may not be fair, but it's how it is.

A Grab Bag of Advice

In graduate school, spend your time working toward publication. Everything else is secondary. After the prestige of your department, the most important determinant of whether you'll get a job is how much and how well you publish.

Remember that your goal is to get a job. You should act strategically to ensure that you graduate with an impressive, stand-out CV that screams "hire me." A good graduate program helps you get a job. A good advisor helps you get a job.

Start by doing backward induction. Ask yourself, to get a job in my fifth year, what does my CV need to look like then? For me to have a competitive CV in year 5, what do I need to do during year 4? To be able to do that in year 4, what do I need to do in year 3? Go all the way back to the present day. You'll realize your job search begins on the very first day of your first year of graduate school. Start doing what it takes. You are training for the Olympics, remember. First place means a wonderful job for life; second place means you leave academia.

Take a close look at recent graduates from your programs who got jobs. (If there aren't any such students, quit or transfer.) What did their CVs look like when they graduated? How did they spend their time in grad school? Email them and ask them for advice. Ask their professors how the students did it. Emulate and copy their behavior. The job market is getting worse, so do better than they did.

When picking an advisor, pick someone whose students consistently get jobs. Pick an advisor who understands the market and wants you to succeed; don't just pick the most famous person in your department or the person whose interests best match yours—unless that person helps her students get jobs. I've had colleagues who, despite being successful themselves, constantly gave their students bad advice, such as "don't publish in grad school."

By the way, if your advisor contradicts the advice I give in this book, this might mean your subfield is unusual, or it might instead mean your advisor doesn't understand what the job market is like nowadays. If your advisor's students don't regularly get jobs, you know which it is.

A good rule of thumb: You can't get any job your advisor couldn't get. If your advisor wouldn't be competitive for a job at Princeton, then neither will you.

Avoid selecting an advisor who doesn't care about her students, who wants students to become his disciples, or who doesn't tolerate intellectual disagreement. If Professor Smith's students tend to write dissertations of the form "Here's what Prof. Smith would have said about X if only he'd written on it," that's a red flag. First, you're more likely to burn out and hate your life if you become someone else's mouthpiece. Second, hiring committees want to hire original thinkers. You don't want your work to be seen as derivative. Third, many hiring committees don't care what Smith really would have said about X, let alone what his students think he would have said. Remember that your department is not the profession. Unless you are literally enrolled in the top three to five departments, then what your department or professors find especially interesting may be of little interest to the general profession. Anything you write about, whether for your dissertation or your seminar papers, should be of interest to large numbers of people in the profession. Ideally, it should be interesting to lots of people outside the profession too.

When taking graduate seminars, don't write seminar papers. Write articles. Your goal is not to get an A in the class or to validate your professor. Your goal is to use that seminar to help you publish a paper in a prestigious journal.

Ask the professor for the reading assignments before the class begins. Do half the reading over summer or winter break. Start drafting your seminar paper in the first week of class. Spend the semester revising the paper as you learn more. Have your professor and others read and critique it. Present it at professional conferences. Once you finish the semester, you can and should have a polished paper ready to submit to journals.

You should aim to have at least two good publications in indisputable top-level journals when you graduate. These journals often have acceptance rates under 5%. To accomplish this task, you'll need to start submitting your papers for consideration almost right away.

On this point, here's an excellent policy I learned from the economists Tyler Cowen and Mike Munger: Starting in your second year of graduate school, and at least until you receive tenure, try to have *three papers under review* at all times. I realize this is demanding advice, and I'm not saying it's necessary or sufficient to succeed. However, if you can pull it off, your chances of success—in getting a job and earning tenure—will be much higher.

If a paper gets rejected, read the comments, revise it slightly if the comments are actually useful, then resubmit it right away. If you always have three papers under review, you'll probably end up with an impressive CV, and then a job, and then tenure.

The time to start publishing is *now*. Really, it was yesterday, but you can't do anything about that. You can't wait until your fourth or fifth year to start trying to publish. You might need to spend two or three years revising and modifying a paper until it is finally accepted by a good journal. Journals often take six months or a year to decide whether to accept a paper. You might have a paper rejected four or five times before it's accepted. To have a couple of papers published in top journals by year 5 means having five papers out for review in year 3.

The biggest secret to publishing is to actually take the shot. Sure, there are things you can do to make it more or less likely that you'll be accepted or rejected. But the main thing is to take the shot. You need to get over the fear of rejection. You need to avoid thinking, "I don't want to know whether I'm good enough, so I won't submit anything." You need to avoid thinking, "I shouldn't submit this until it's perfect." Take the shot. You'd be surprised at how many graduate students self-sabotage; they don't submit papers because they fear rejection letters.

Teach, but Not Too Much

I've already explained how to use your time as a TA productively. When you sit in on your professor's lectures, you should spend that time preparing your own version of that same or closely related classes. In grad school, you might be able to finish all the prep you'll need for your first few years as a professor.

If you can, it's good to teach a few classes on your own, as an independent instructor. You want to show search committees you've got the chops. Ideally, you should teach a range of courses, including courses outside your specialty. If you specialize in labor economics, everyone assumes you can teach that, so prove to them you can also teach econometrics or intermediate microeconomics. If you specialize in physical chemistry, prove you can teach biochemistry.

Remember, while PhD-granting departments might have thirty professors who only teach in their subfield, the typical college professor works in a tiny department and must be able to teach nearly every class the department offers. You'll want to show hiring committees you can do that.

Before you teach, ask the successful teachers how they do it, and then emulate them. Do a good job. But don't overprepare and don't let teaching get in the way of writing and publishing.

Another good rule of thumb: For every hour you spend in the classroom teaching, you shouldn't spend more than two hours outside the classroom on preparation, grading, and other activities. The first time you teach a course, if it's far outside your expertise, you can grant yourself a little more leeway. But in general, if you take much more time than that, you're setting yourself up to fail. When you're a professor, you'll need to teach more classes, do service work, give talks, and write papers for publication. You must learn to teach well with minimal outside work.

Don't Date Other Graduate Students

If you're the kind of person who wants a PhD, you're a weirdo. You love talking about ideas and concepts. You want to debate theories. You enjoy abstract thinking and analysis. You might find what normal people talk about boring and unbearable. You're a nerd who likes nerdy things. For that reason, your perfect romantic partner may well be another weirdo like you. Other graduate students "get it." They understand what you're going through, and they think like you.

Here's some harsh advice, though: All things considered, dating other graduate students is a bad idea. The reason it's a bad idea is because they're such good matches for you. You might fall in love and want to stay together in the long term, in a marriage or other committed relationship.

I'm not recommending that you dump your current boyfriend or girlfriend. Finding real love is almost as hard as finding an academic job. But if you're single, consider expanding your social circle to include people outside academia, especially professionals with highly mobile jobs.

The problem with dating another grad student is that when you go on the market, you'll then suffer from the "two-body problem." It's hard enough for you to get any job you might apply for. If you manage to get an offer in the classics department at East Tennessee State, you'll then have to ask/beg the deans to hire your spouse/partner in the psych department. Even for a rock-star senior academic, that's a hard ask. As a junior person, you're lucky enough to get any job, let alone be able to ask your employer to hire your partner. I've seen it happen, but it is unusual. Keep in mind that the other department may not want your spouse—no matter how qualified he or she is— because they worry they would lose a potential hire down the road. Spousal hires are expensive and require lots of special favors exchanged between deans and departments.

When you graduate, you probably won't get to choose where in the country or world you live. It's rare to get one job offer, let alone two. The chances that both you and your partner would be independently hired at the same university, or even in the same geographic area, are slim. So, there's a good chance that the first spouse to get a job will end up asking the second spouse to sacrifice his or her career to stay together. Or, you might be stuck in a long-distance relationship. Your partner gets a job in LA and you find one in rural Iowa. It's rough.

Life is short, so love the one you got. But if you haven't got anybody, trying dating outside academia.

Networking Is Crucial

In graduate school, it's easy to treat your own graduate department as if it were the entire world. You worry about pleasing the professors, having a good reputation in the department, being a good citizen, being friends with the other students, and so on.

But your department isn't going to hire you. Next time they have a tenure-track opening, they'll try to hire someone from a better-ranked department than their own. Your tenth-ranked program will hire someone from the #1 program. Your ability to get a job depends in large part on having a good reputation in the field. So, it's smart to cultivate allies and friends in other institutions.

In academia, networking is vital, especially for graduate students and new PhDs. Remember that in most fields, even the least desirable jobs (in terms of pay, quality of life, school reputation, student quality) get hundreds of applications from people who would be grateful to land such positions. The faculty at those schools—many of whom are teaching four classes a semester while trying to do research and service, and maintain a personal life—are looking for ways to narrow those hundreds of applications down to the ten or so applicants they'll actually interview. Having a stand-out CV—filled with teaching awards and impressive publications—certainly helps.

It also helps if the faculty already know you. Perhaps they've heard of you from a friend, or they've already read your published work. Perhaps they saw you give excellent comments on a paper at a regional or national conference. Perhaps they've seen you present your own work at such conferences. Perhaps you had some email correspondence with them about some of their papers a few years before. Perhaps you had dinner with them when you met at some conference.

Remember, faculty aren't just trying to hire another teacher or researcher in their department. They know that anyone they hire might be their colleague for thirty years or more. They want to hire someone they respect and whose company they enjoy. They want someone they can discuss ideas with, go to lunch with, and who will read their papers or substitute in their classes when they need help.

Networking is strategic, but to be strategic in your networking, you want to avoid being too strategic. Here's what I mean: There are plenty of graduate students and young assistant professors who go out of their way to meet as many people as possible. Some of them come across as smarmy. Their intentions are too obvious. I've known a few grad students who, every time I interacted with them, came across as users. (They knew I was on the hiring committee of a prestigious postdoc, and it was obvious they were buttering me up to help their chances.)

The key is to network but not to be fake. Don't be a user; just be a good colleague who gets out there and participates in public events. Attend—and present at—events and conferences. Be polite and gracious. Say smart things. Network, but don't put networking at the forefront of your thoughts. Nail your presentations. Ask smart questions. Admit when you're wrong or uncertain. Be collegial and be present. If you go to lots of public events and do a good job, you'll network the right way as a side effect. You should do these things anyway, because they're part of what it means to be an academic.

It may well turn out that the reason *you* got a job over the other thirty or so people with equally impressive CVs is that the hiring professors already knew you and liked you. They selected you because you were a sure thing.

Writing Your Dissertation

There's a saying I've heard dozens of times—it's even on Twitter. I don't know who came up with it, but here's how it goes:

> A good dissertation is a done dissertation. A good dissertation is a published dissertation. A perfect dissertation is neither.

You might think, huh? Isn't the whole point of grad school to write a good dissertation? Answer: No, the point of grad school is to get a job.

A dissertation is a school project. It's a long school project that might take you a year or two to write (if you do it right) or many years to write (if you do it wrong), but that's all it is. If your dissertation is merely a dissertation, maybe four people will read it: you and your three graduate committee members. Don't even count on your committee reading the whole thing.

It should be good enough to pass. But it shouldn't be perfect.

For most students, the real goal, when writing the dissertation, is to produce *stand-alone* publishable articles—and publish them. You should have at least one or two dissertation chapters that can be excerpted, presented, and published independently in peer-reviewed journals. Maybe your department requires you to write the dissertation as a long-form book, but nevertheless—unless you're in certain humanities fields (e.g., history) where books are the primary form of academic output—you should use this time to ensure that you have two papers you can present and publish. You don't need a perfect dissertation; you need two good articles or chapters.

The rest of the dissertation doesn't have to be perfect. It's not even worth trying to make it perfect. After you graduate, no one will read it. You need the dissertation to be good enough that you can talk through the rest of it and answer questions about it during interviews, but even a hiring committee that offers you a job will not read your dissertation. In reality, you'll probably only ever discuss the one chapter you submitted as a writing sample in your application—if even that.

This isn't being lazy. After all, in most of academia, the standard form of publication isn't a dissertation, but a journal article. In some parts of academia, say in English, history, or philosophy, publishing scholarly books is as prestigious as— even more prestigious than—publishing in journals. But even then, the typical dissertation doesn't read like a book, and it's not even very good training for writing a book. It is possible to turn your dissertation into a book, but this usually requires massive revisions after you graduate, when you've had more practice writing for peer-reviewed publication rather than writing to please your professors.

If your supervisor disagrees—if she insists that every little bit be perfect, at the expense of helping you produce publishable articles—then your advisor may be (unintentionally) hurting you. Consider getting a new advisor. Remember, if your advisor kills your career, he still gets to keep his job, make his mortgage payments, and keep chugging along. You're the one who suffers the consequences.

If you follow my advice on writing productively (see chapter 3), you should generally have no trouble finishing and defending your dissertation by the end of your fifth year. Yes, there are exceptions to that rule—there are some projects that really do take five years to do well. However, most students who say they need five years in reality aren't writing productively.

If you struggle to finish your dissertation, you probably aren't going to succeed as a professor. You should consider quitting, or finishing but pursuing a nonacademic career. There's nothing wrong with that. This job isn't for everyone, and that's fine.

I realize that seems harsh. But consider: When you write your dissertation, you aren't taking classes. You'll either continue to be a teaching assistant for one class, or perhaps get to teach your own class. You'll have almost zero responsibility other than writing your dissertation. That's your full-time job. If you can't hack that in a year, then how will you manage to be productive in research when—as an assistant professor—you also have to teach four to eight classes and perform service work, all without anyone mentoring you or holding your hand? In terms of responsibilities, grad school is the easiest time in your career. The years you spend writing your dissertation are the years with the fewest responsibilities. It doesn't get better.

By the way, some students choose to take extra classes even though they aren't required to do so. Before you do that, remember that taking extra classes won't get you a job. Producing good, published research will. Hiring committees want to hire colleagues, not professional students. If taking an extra class will help you publish more or better, then do it. Otherwise, don't.

Finish. Don't Take Your Time

The median graduate student takes seven and a half years to finish a PhD. In some fields—oddly, in the fields with the worst job prospects—they take longer.

Longer is bad.

Longer is bad because time is a price. Imagine you want to ride a roller coaster. The roller coaster stays the same no matter how long you wait in line. If you wait in line for an hour, you pay a higher price for that ride than the otherwise identical person who waited only fifteen minutes. His expected "profit"—the benefits minus the costs—exceeds yours. The same goes for getting a job. Better to get the job now—and start making real money, having kids, saving for retirement, getting real respect, having money to travel, or whatnot—than six years from now.

Further, if you're going to fail to get a job, better to fail sooner than later. The sooner you determine you won't make it in academia, the sooner you can pursue plan B.

Longer is also bad because time-to-PhD is a signal. Your CV tells a story. The time it takes you to earn a PhD tells a story. All things being equal, the longer you take, the more your CV communicates "inefficient, slow, undisciplined, unskilled, won't succeed." Maybe it shouldn't, but it does. If you take five years to write a dissertation, you signal to potential employers that you won't be able to earn tenure.

Remember, hiring committees want to hire a colleague who they think can hack it. They want someone who clearly signals they can handle the workload with ease and grace. They want to hire someone who will publish consistently and at a high level, who will excel in teaching, and will do her part as a citizen of the university.

So, imagine we have two candidates. One finished in five years with three publications. The other finished in ten years with no publications. We have very strong evidence that the first applicant is better than the second. The second one had far less responsibility than any of us does and yet managed to produce far less than what we expect of someone in seven years of full-time work. Unless there's a good excuse—like a serious illness—we have strong evidence that the second student won't earn tenure. Into the discard pile his application goes.

We aren't being mean. We're doing the student a favor.

We all know there are exceptions to these norms. Some people have projects that are ambitious and worthwhile but take five years to complete. Some people have personal conflicts that explain their time to PhD. People on hiring committees know this and want to accommodate these sorts of cases. However, remember that committees are probably spending a minute per CV on the first round. Unless it's somehow obvious why you took so long, or unless you're highly impressive in other ways, a long time-to-PhD will hurt you.

UPSHOTS

- Your chances of getting a job depend on how you approach graduate school.
- You need to engage in reverse induction. Figure out what you need to do to be competitive when you go on the market, and work backward from there.
- Getting into grad schools depends on undergrad school prestige, grades, GRE scores, and writing samples. Students from elite research schools have greater success than others.
- PhD programs generally require two to three years of classes, followed by qualifying and prospectus exams, followed by writing and defending a dissertation.
- Go to the highest-ranked program you can. High-ranked programs dominate most job markets.
- Before choosing a program, look at the placement rates of its graduates and at the kinds of jobs its students get; if you're an average student, those are the kinds of jobs you'll get.
- You can increase your job prospects by choosing the right field. You can study the same issues in economics and political science, but all things being equal, you will have better prospects in economics.
- Publish as much as you can in good journals as a grad student. Students with good publication records have much better chances of getting jobs.
- Most PhD students take more than seven years to graduate, but you should aim for five—and it's not hard to do that if you have good time-management skills.
- Never take on debt to get a PhD. Only go to a university that waives tuition and gives a living stipend.
- You can use your time as a teaching assistant—including hours spent in your professors' lectures—to prep your own courses and teaching materials; when you leave grad school, you can easily have five to ten classes ready to go.
- Don't spend more than five hours a week on the modal week on class prep. Spend your time doing research. Most TAs overprepare.
- Use each class to write a peer-reviewed publication, not a seminar paper.
- Starting your second year of grad school and at least until you have tenure, aim to have three papers under review at all times.
- Networking is crucial for getting a job. Don't be smarmy—just present papers at conferences and volunteer to comment on others' papers.
- A good dissertation is a done dissertation. A dissertation is a school project.

THREE

How to Be Productive and Happy

BETWEEN COLLEGE AND GRADUATE SCHOOL, I worked as an automobile insurance adjustor. It was honest, honorable work, though rather boring. I'd say the same about the other odd jobs I've had: implant operator at a microchip factory, computer chassis assembler, various jobs at a bakery, and so on.

These jobs had another thing in common: When I went home for the night, I was finished. When I left Analog Devices' parking lot, I never had a nagging thought that I should ionize more argon. When I punched out at Market Basket, I didn't fret about whether I should fry more donuts. On weekends home from GEICO's offices, I didn't worry about all the auto claims I missed. When work was over, it was over.

Academia feels different. No matter how much you do, there is always more to do. You could spend more time writing. You could read new books for erudition or to help spark research ideas of your own. Each month, hundreds of new articles and books appear in your narrow research area—shouldn't you read that stuff? Wouldn't it be irresponsible not to? You could brainstorm new pedagogical methods or develop and improve your courses. You could sit in on star teachers' courses to learn their techniques. You could spend more time grading papers and providing students with feedback. You could attend workshops on teaching methods. You could invent new programs for students or attend any of the dozens of events the average college hosts each week.

In academia, when you go home for the night or wake up Saturday morning, it's tempting to ask yourself, "Why aren't you writing?" When a book or paper is accepted for publication, it's tempting to think, "Great, but what's *next*?"

Academic jobs are like ideal gasses. They expand to fill as much time as we allow them. There is always more work to do, more to grade, more to prep, more students to advise, more to read, more to write.

Academia can be a high-pressure job, in which people must juggle multiple and conflicting responsibilities and constant deadlines, as well as work toward long-term goals with distant completion dates. The more successful you are (on certain measures), the more people will ask you to do things for them. You'll be asked to write papers for anthologies, give talks, attend conferences, referee papers, referee research grants, chair committees, and more. People will request almost a year's worth of extra work from you each year.

The philosopher Derek Parfit—one of the most important philosophers of the twentieth century—had a "monomaniacal commitment to philosophy"; "throughout his adult life he did little other than think about, read, and write philosophy."[1] For decades he lived a "monk-like existence."[2] He ate the same Spartan meals every day.

I don't know whether Parfit was happy. I don't know whether in his case, the trade-offs were worth it. Perhaps he would have been as productive and produced the same quality work if he'd taken more weekends off, had children, or lived a more varied lifestyle. I don't know. But I suspect most of us wouldn't flourish if we tried to live the way Parfit lived. Most of us would burn out. We would make our domestic partners and friends burn out and resent us. We'd be absent from our kids' lives, if we have them. We'd have no hobbies.

Academic success isn't worthwhile success if it makes you miserable. One of the easiest ways for it to make you miserable is to let it swallow every waking moment. That's true even if you love your work, as I do. Consider, by extension: You may love your hobbies, but if you did your hobbies for eighty hours a week year after year, you'd probably grow to hate them—and your life—too.

The good news is that happiness is something one can *plan* for. Both happiness and success in academia are largely a product of good time management. Happy academics learn to get enough done without working thirty-five hundred hours a year. It sounds clichéd, but the key is to work smarter, not longer.

I spend a great deal of this chapter discussing productivity in research, but I also cover teaching and service. Because I realize most faculty spend most of their time teaching, that focus may be puzzling. Here's my reasoning: Everyone has to do some research, even teaching-focused faculty. Learning to do it efficiently is a bigger mystery than learning to teach efficiently. Graduate students, in particular, looking to get jobs, don't have time to learn research productivity through trial and error. In contrast, many learn to teach in grad school because their time spent teaching provides them with some close-to-immediate feedback mechanisms. They see firsthand how students respond.

Your Job Is a Job

Remember that an academic job is just a job. You agree to produce certain kinds of outputs and do certain things in exchange for money. Just as I didn't work overtime at GEICO or Market Basket for free, I don't work overtime at Georgetown for free. When I was an insurance adjustor, I did my job well, but I kept it in its proper place. The same goes for being a professor, even though I love my job now. (Most of it, anyway.)

There is a time for academic work and a time for other things. Just as you don't let your hobbies intrude into your work time, you don't let your work intrude into your hobby time. I recommend that you set explicit parameters and then adhere to them. Decide up front how many hours a week you want to spend on academic work. Create—and write down, at least at first—a time budget. Allocate hours to different tasks. Stick to your numbers.

Since this is a genuine budget, this means you must prioritize some things over others and cut out some things entirely. Consider that if you have, say, $7,500 a month in cash to spend, you know you have to take care of necessities first. You can't buy everything you want when you want it. You have to forgo some pleasures and luxuries. You have to save up for certain things—a trip, a new car, a new road bicycle. The same goes for time. You have every right to choose to work forty hours a week. You don't owe it to the profession, the university, or your students to work sixty hours a week, fifty weeks a year.[3]

Once you've got your time budget, it requires you—and enables you—to spend time on the necessities and cut out the less important things. Many things are in some sense worth doing, but they exceed your time budget. You'll have to decide, given that you're going to work forty hours a week, what the best way is to spend that time.

Try to avoid going into "debt" by exceeding your time budget. If you must work extra time this week, then balance your books by taking time off work next week. If you must stay late to judge a case competition on Thursday, then go home early on Friday or don't come in at all. If you need to work a Saturday morning and, as a result, miss time with your kids, then do something special or extra with them Thursday afternoon.

Understanding Diminishing Marginal Returns

Many profiles of Derek Parfit say he had a single-minded obsession with perfecting his work. He didn't want his work to be great, but perfect. In my opinion, and I suspect in his, he didn't achieve perfection. While his work is brilliant, important, and highly regarded, there's no guarantee people will read it fifty or a hundred years from now. I was never asked to read any of it in my undergraduate or graduate school days, and I don't recall refereeing a paper that cites it recently.

Regardless, it's worth asking whether perfection is ever the point. Perfection in any endeavor is almost never worth the price you pay for it.

A basic and fundamental finding in economics is that most things have *diminishing marginal returns*. This means that, all things being equal, the first unit of something is worth more than the next, which is worth more than the next. Each additional unit you input or consume is worth a little less than the one before it.

For example, suppose you're starving. That first bag of rice saves your life. The next bag gives you some security. But suppose I keep handing you bags of rice, minute after minute. By the time I give you the hundredth bag of rice, you might use the rice for low-value things, such as throwing it at newlyweds, making crafts, or building cool rice-bag paintball forts. At some point, you run out of space to store the extra rice. The next bag has *negative* value. At some further point, you'd be willing to pay me to stop dumping rice bags on your front lawn.

The same goes for eating the rice. The first cup at dinner feeds you. The second cup is enjoyable but makes you feel stuffed. The third cup makes you sick. The fourth ruptures your stomach.

This also goes for hiring, say, customer service personnel at GEICO. Each additional worker is worth a bit less than the last one. At some point, if you keep adding workers, you end up paying the next worker more than the value he produces for your company. You lose money on that hire.

This works for professors, too. You might love to have more colleagues, but do you have the space or need for another forty people in your department? What would they even teach? Would they just make faculty meetings impossible?

Figure 3.1 illustrates how the concept of diminishing marginal returns applies to your workweek. On average, the first hour you spend writing, or preparing a class, or grading a paper, is more productive and valuable than the next, which is in turn more valuable than the next.

When you arrive at point A, you start to experience sharply diminishing returns. You keep improving that manuscript, you

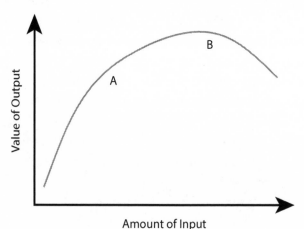

Figure 3.1. Diminishing marginal returns.

keep adding good comments to the student's paper, you keep learning more about some new concept, but the value per hour spent becomes ever smaller.

For instance, I notice that once I've spent about four hours writing, I can keep working, but not as effectively. The sentences come out more slowly. I have more difficulty thinking through puzzles. Each sentence takes more effort. I feel as if I'm swimming through honey rather than water. That's the point where I stop writing and turn to the other things my job requires.

When you arrive at point B, you start having negative returns. Perhaps you're at the point where it's taking you three hours to make one small revision. Perhaps the last hour of prep for your class produced hardly any actual value. Perhaps—and this is the real threat—you've overworked yourself. You're too tired and your brain's too fried to do good work. You need to rest, rejuvenate, and take care of your other needs.

The upshot: As you get past point A, you should strongly consider doing something else, whether it's a different form of work or some form of leisure. If you get to point B, you need to stop entirely—your additional effort is making your work *worse*.

Here's another way to think of this. Since you get diminishing marginal benefits from each additional hour of work, you also thereby incur *increasing* marginal *costs*. That's a general phenomenon for any kind of production.

For instance, suppose your university wants to make your campus pristine. They want to remove all extra filth and litter from the campus. The first few hours the custodial staff spends cleaning may be amazingly productive—the bathrooms go from disgusting to acceptable, the garbage gets emptied, the leaves get raked. But suppose the college president wants to remove literally every piece of litter from campus. It might take

$5 million in labor and resources to locate and remove that last wad of gum or cigarette butt hidden out there.

Figure 3.2 illustrates this concept. As the quantity of an input increases, the marginal benefits decrease and the marginal costs increase. In the abstract, the rational stopping point is where these two curves intersect. If you're to the left of the intersection, you can get additional value by scaling up. If you're to the right of the intersection, the costs of your additional activities exceed your marginal benefits. It's time to scale back.

One reason why marginal costs increase is that the more time you spend on one thing, the more you must give up to keep doing that thing. Your costs rise because your opportunity costs rise. The more time you spend working, the more you give up relaxing, going to movies, having a hobby, getting enough sleep, maintaining or having friendships, being with a spouse or children, and more.

The upshot: Determine, in your case, where MB = MC. That's your work-time budget. That's your stopping point. Working past the point where MB = MC isn't dedication; it's

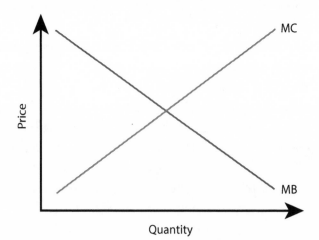

Figure 3.2. Marginal benefit and marginal cost.

waste. Maybe for Derek Parfit, where MB = MC was ninety hours a week. Maybe it is for you, too. However, I suspect most who think so are kidding themselves.

Busy Is Beside the Point

Every conversation in the elevator:
"Hey, how's your semester going?"
"Oh, you know how it is. Busy, busy, busy."
Academia is a cult of busy. Ask people what's up, and they'll say busy. Sometimes they say that to preempt you from asking a favor. But even when they know that's not coming, that's what they say. They say that in part because they are indeed busy. But another part of the reason is that many people regard *looking* or *being* busy as evidence that they are important, useful, contributing, or doing their share.

That's a mistake. Busy is beside the point. Remember that the labor theory of value is false.

As a professor, in the long run, you will be judged by your outputs, not your inputs. If you publish five articles a year in the top three journals in your field, no one will care that you work only fourteen hundred hours a year. If you work three thousand hours a year but publish nothing, no one will care that you worked so much.

Busy is not a badge of honor. Being busy is a cost. When busy translates into good outputs, it's worth the sacrifice. Otherwise, it's a waste. If you aren't accomplishing much, then why are you so busy?

Self-Discipline Is Key

Many undergraduates are smart enough to get As by writing papers the night before they're due. That kind of stuff doesn't cut it in grad school, and it certainly doesn't cut it in academia. Writing a routine undergrad paper is one thing. Writing original work that can sustain peer review in a journal with a 5% acceptance rate is another.

Just as success in grad school requires backward induction, so does academic success in general. If you want to have a paper published in a good journal in year N, you'll need to have a solid working paper to present at seminars in year N-minus-1, which means you need to actively write it in N-minus-2, which means you need to collect data in N-minus-3. If you need six articles and a book to get tenure, then you need to be working on those six articles and the book pretty soon after starting your tenure-track job.

Some people say they work best under pressure. It's an illusion. No one works best under pressure. Instead, some people *trick* themselves into thinking they do because they *choose only to work* under pressure. What's better than working under pressure is working and being productive without pressure or stress. The key to that is being disciplined about your work.

On any given day, you'll encounter a conflict between what's most urgent and what's most important. To illustrate, let's say you're a research-focused tenure-line professor, like me. I get something like seventy to a hundred emails a day, each demanding my attention and asking me to perform some task or do some favor. I have office hours, classes, and committee meetings. I have manuscripts to referee, recommendation letters to write, job candidates to assess. I could redo my PowerPoint slides or read new stuff to assign for student reading.

Or let's say you're a graduate student, which means you should be focusing on your research above all else. You have your own list of conflicts. The students in your sections email you, asking you to hold extra office hours at weird times, to explain a concept to them, to ask you questions that are already answered on the syllabus they didn't read, or to outline what happened in the class they missed. ("Did we cover anything important while I was gone?") Other grad students email to suggest you run for graduate student government. (P.S. Don't do that.)

Success means ensuring that you focus most of your time, and especially your most productive time, on what's *important* rather than what's *urgent*. If you always do what's urgent first, you won't do what's important—or enough of it, at least.

One way to solve this problem is to write every morning for, say, three hours, before you do any other kind of work. Write first, when your brain is freshest and you have the most energy. Then answer emails, prep for class, hold office hours, and so on. If you can, get your courses scheduled for the afternoon. Or, at the very least, try to have all your courses scheduled on certain days of the week, so you can spend other days writing full time.

Maybe for you research isn't the priority. My point generalizes: Pick what's most important, and do that first, before you feel worn out.

Maybe you're not a morning person. I wasn't until I had children. So a more general strategy is to determine when you do your best work, and then make sure you spend that time, each working day, on whatever is most important. Say no to things that interfere with your using your best time on what's important. For instance, I was a night person until my late twenties, and so I would be sure to spend, say, 11 p.m. until 2 a.m. writing each work night. That meant I couldn't watch David Letterman in his best years. So be it.

I mentioned before that good discipline means not overspending your time budget. It also means making sure you spend all of your budget. For a research-focused professor or a graduate student, I recommend spending twenty hours a week writing. If you're not already doing so, it's worth keeping an actual log of how much you are writing. Figure out when you write and what's getting in the way. Make sure you hit twenty hours each week.

Writing means writing. When I recommend twenty hours a week writing, I mean working on the paper directly. Editing is writing. Writing a new draft or a new sentence is writing. Reading something new for the sake of helping your writing is not writing. Talking about the paper with others is not writing, though you should do that, too.

Write down how you actually spend your time, then examine your budget at the end of each week. Ask: Is there a difference between how I planned to spend my time and how I actually spent it? Am I underinvesting in certain things? Did I spend time on things that in retrospect I should have skipped—or reduced? Where did I misinvest my time? Is there a conflict I could have avoided? Could I be more productive if I rearranged when I do this or that? How could I reallocate my time better? What did I do well and what do I need to change?

This may seem banal, but it works. It's similar to the advice dietitians give their patients. Some patients could reduce their overeating and eat better if they simply kept track of and reviewed how much and what they actually ate.[4] In the heat of the moment, it's easy to eat too many M&Ms and not think of it again. Do the same day after day and you're on track for diabetes. But if you read at the end of the week that you ate three bags of M&Ms, you'll probably find a way to change. Discipline is key, but discipline requires self-awareness.

Being disciplined about research or teaching productivity is an ongoing commitment. It means adopting productive habits and sticking to them. You could try to write in spurts, perhaps by going months writing nothing, only to try to pop out a book in three months. But that's a recipe for a mixture of guilt and stress. You'll feel guilt and shame during the unproductive months. You'll feel growing stress as the deadline approaches and you've got nothing going. You'll feel tremendous stress when you overwork yourself to meet the deadline—plus guilt for the way you neglect your spouse and friends when you condense a year's worth of work into three months. When the book doesn't live up to your hopes, you'll feel guilt knowing you would have done better work had you spread it out.

Earn Rewards, Then Take Them

Here are two pieces of advice:[5]

1 Earn breaks, then take them.
2 Earn rewards, then take them.

We've covered the first point to some degree already. If you're like most people, you won't remain productive as an academic unless you take regular breaks, which allow you to feel refreshed. You should aim to take time off during each workday to work out, walk around, eat lunch. You should aim to take every weekend off and also aim to have spent your working week with sufficient discipline that you never feel "guilty" about that.

Do whatever it takes to make it a joy to get out of bed each morning. Rewarding yourself for your accomplishments helps keep you fresh and happy. Having a concrete reward can help you feel that your successes are tangible and real.

Perhaps this means making certain deals with yourself. If you accomplish a goal, you get some reward. For a small thing—like finishing a draft of a dissertation chapter—you might go out for a nice lunch or dinner. Getting a paper accepted might entail, among other things, taking the rest of the week off to play golf. For me, getting a new book published or getting a promotion has sometimes meant giving myself permission to buy a nice guitar or amplifier. For you, it might be that when you get a tenure-track job offer, tenure, or win the university teaching award, you allow yourself to take your dream vacation.

Figure out what your rewards are. Set a reasonable goal to qualify for one of them. Then work for it.

Picking a Research Topic and Finding Ideas

Many grad students and young academics fear they will get to a point where they don't know what to write about. What if I run out of ideas? What if I can't come up with something for a dissertation topic?

In general, I'm not worried about that. Everyone has good ideas. Grad students who fail often have good ideas. The real trouble is turning a good idea into a publishable paper or acceptable dissertation. That said, everyone gets stuck once in a while.

Here are some strategies for coming up with ideas: Look for unanswered questions. Perhaps, at the end of a seminal paper or book, some major theorist asks but doesn't answer some hard question about her own theory. Answer that question.

1 Do certain major papers contain questionable assumptions or premises?
2 Both A and B seem to be true, but they can't both be true. How do we resolve that? If we can't find a way to square A and B, which should we give up?
3 Do three distinct theories turn out to be the same idea?
4 Does your academic field often make presumptions about certain things that another academic field has

challenged or falsified? (For instance, I noticed that when philosophers defend democracy, they often rely upon models of voter behavior that political scientists and economists have shown to be false.)

5 Read work outside your academic field. If you're an economist, read sociology and anthropology. You may find brand new ideas you can use for new purposes. Perhaps some anthropologist has hypothesized that P, but as an economist, you can produce a more rigorous test of that hypothesis. Perhaps P solves some puzzle economists haven't solved on their own.

6 Do certain major theories lead to predictions or have implications the field or the theorists don't wish to endorse? Might certain theories make false predictions or have perverse implications?

7 Read major papers and look for the words *obviously*, *clearly*, and *of course* in front of sentences. Ask yourself, are the things the authors say are clear and obvious actually clear and obvious? Or are these instead unfounded assumptions someone—like you—should challenge? Do people take for granted things they shouldn't take for granted?

8 What's one part of commonsense, conventional wisdom—the kind of thing laypeople believe—that is probably false? What's something that's probably true but that no one has yet rigorously tested?

9 Is there an idea from one part of your field that applies to things in another part of the field?

10 Ask yourself: Is my topic interesting to people outside academia? Could I explain what I'm working on to my hairdresser or auto mechanic in a way that they'd find intriguing? If not, that may be a sign you're working on a project that doesn't really matter. It may

take a PhD and specialized training to do your work, but it shouldn't, in general, take a PhD and specialized training to care about it.

11 When people in your field argue for X and against Y, do they apply different standards? Do they change assumptions in self-serving ways? Do they demand more evidence for what they don't want to believe than they do for what they want to believe?

Another bit of advice is to write for the ages.[6] The point isn't just to get something—anything—published. It's to work on work that is worth doing and worth reading. On this point, economist Mike Munger says:

"What are you writing that will be read ten years from now? What about 100 years from now?" Having gotten the question myself, I can tell you it is pretty intimidating. And embarrassing, because most of us don't think that way (which is another reason most people don't get nominated for the Nobel Prize). Young scholars focus on "getting published" as if it had nothing to do with ideas, or the importance of your arguments. Paradoxically, if all you are trying to do is "get published," you may not publish very much. If you write important papers about profound problems, the publishing will take care of itself.[7]

Many graduate students write papers of the form "Here's what I think my supervisor would have said about X had she written about it" or "Here's my response to footnote 534 of *Big Seminal Book from Twenty Years Ago*." Others end up doing routine, boring normal science. There's a role for such work, to be sure, but it's difficult to build a rewarding career out of being a follower and a second-hander.

There's a strategic point in writing for the ages, too. Working on big ideas means more people will read you and respond to you. It means you'll have higher citation counts—which matters for tenure and promotion. It means you're likelier to get paid speaking invitations or be able to turn your journal article into a royalty-producing book. It also means you'll have more satisfaction with your job, because you'll feel that your work matters.

There's some tension here between these various bits of advice. I've argued that you should not aim for perfection, but now I'm arguing that you should write for the ages. It's not exactly a contradiction—the great stuff we read from fifty or a hundred years ago is imperfect, so great does not equal perfect. But there is a seeming tension here between idealistic advice about shooting for the stars and pragmatic advice about just getting stuff done and out.

Here's how I resolve that tension. First, if you've got a small idea that you can easily write up and get published, go ahead. But, second, the big ideas are the ones that sustain you. You might invent a new concept or come up with something big, and that big idea will carry you for five years or more. It will become ten papers, not just one. It will make people notice you and respect you in a way a small bit of "normal science" won't. And it will be more fun.

Aiming to write stuff people will read one hundred years from now is demanding, and most of us with this goal won't succeed. But by aiming that high, we at least succeed in doing work worth reading ten years from now. If you only aim to do something worth reading today, you probably won't achieve even that. In short: Shoot for the stars and maybe you'll at least hit the moon.

You might think it's unfair that you have to pick an "interesting" topic. You might think your topic is intrinsically interesting, so others should be as interested in it as you are. But here's an analogy to dispel that notion.[8] Suppose you hear two people talking about baseball. You think baseball is boring and soccer is better. So you bust in and say, "Hey, did you see Manchester United last night?" How do you think you'd be received?

Maybe your dissertation is on seventeenth-century avant-garde Romanian poetry, but no one's talking about it. I'm not saying your topic is bad. But it's your job to get people to want to listen—not their job to want to listen. If you disagree, fine. Think of it this way: They aren't going to decide spontaneously to turn their attention toward you. You'll have to find a way to make them care.

Write First, Read Second

Mike Munger explains why Nobel laureate economist Douglass C. North (Mike's dissertation advisor) would always present messy, half-finished papers instead of waiting until they were polished:

> The first time [North] would present a paper, it would be incomplete, with significant gaps in the argument. Doug is a very smart man, so an incomplete paper by him is still better than a complete paper from most of us, but it always seemed strange to me.
>
> But then I realized what he was doing. It was what a computer programmer would call "machine-intensive debugging": run the job, and see what error messages you get, instead of puzzling out the code all by yourself. Professor North would present his paper, which had the germ of a good idea but needed some more work. One of the people in the audience would say, "Oh, you should read Smith's 1996 book on that, and also the articles by Mbuto and Jones." North would then take the suggestion and incorporate the new ideas. Don't get me wrong;

he fully acknowledged the comments and cited the new books and papers appropriately. My point is that the writing comes first. If you read North's published work, it contains some of the most profound and broad-ranging ideas of the last three decades. Those ideas are all North's, but he wrote them down and then solicited comments on how to make his argument more effectively, and also on how to find other people's work that contained some related ideas.[9]

This approach makes sense. Your paper has a good sketch of a central argument and thesis, but it's buggy. You write the basic code and then stress test it, find the bugs, and fix it. You do the reading, but you read strategically. Instead of "Let me first read everything and then see if I have anything to add," you start with "Here's what I want to say—so now let me read everything directly relevant to my basic argument."

As you read, you revise and edit your original piece. You make notes about other things to look into. You write up a strategy for how to fix your paper. And then you do what you planned. This method ensures that reading helps you produce research and does not come at the expense of research.

You've got an idea for an article, a dissertation, a book. A thought occurs to you: Before I start writing, I should read everything written on that topic, plus all the supplementary and ancillary work needed to understand the most relevant work. Then I'll be an expert and have something to say. It's a completely reasonable thought, but it will kill your career before it gets started. It faces two big problems: First, you'll never run out of stuff to read. Want to write a book on the epistemic foundations of democracy? Great. To read all the articles and books published on that topic just *this year* might take you all year. Want to squeeze in all the classics? Great. That's another twenty years of reading.

A more reasonable version of the "read everything" thought is, "Well, I'd better just read the good stuff." But all the good stuff will cost you a few years, too. You could spend years reading before you write anything. If you are a graduate student or an early career professor, you don't have the time to read without simultaneously producing new research. After all, you're supposed to have three things under review at all times.

The second problem with "read first" is that if you have an idea, that idea is probably vague and undeveloped. If you do a literature search, there's a good chance you'll encounter something that expresses some version of that idea. You'll conclude, alas, that the nascent, undeveloped idea in your head is already out there, already published. But had you written it down into a full essay, you'd probably have produced something original and worth saying. The thing you would have written won't turn out to be the same as the thing you would have read. Your first draft will still need a lot of work, but at least now you have an idea worth developing. You can then read the things you need to read, workshop the paper, and so on, and turn it into a publication.

The "write first, read second" advice applies less to some fields than others. In economics or philosophy, your task is to come up with an original argument. In other fields, such as literature, your task is sometimes with a superior or at least alternative interpretation of existing texts. Still, even in this case, the idea is to read the thing you're interpreting, write out a basic draft of your interpretation, and *then* check the secondary literature. In history, start writing out your interpretation of the facts of some time and place as you read. At the very least, interpret this bit of advice as "Start writing earlier in the process than you normally would; don't wait until you've read everything."

How to Avoid Writer's Block

Many graduate and undergraduate students have writer's block. They have a basic idea of what they want to say, but when they sit down in front of a blank page, the page stays blank for hours. They gnash their teeth and suddenly decide now's the time to organize the garage.

Writer's block often results from a misunderstanding of what writing is. Many people—especially graduate students—think something like this: First, I need to figure out what I want to say. Then, once I've perfected the idea and the phrasing in my head, I put it on the page. The problem is that it's hard to get it perfect in your head, and so you don't get it on the page.

This process is exacerbated by a fear of path dependency: If I don't get it right the first time, then I'll be stuck with it. The definitions won't be quite correct. The examples are not sufficiently apt. The style is wrong. The organization is confused. I need to make sure that the first pass is perfect, or I will have doomed the paper from the start.

You can overcome both problems by following two simple principles:

1 Writing is thinking.
2 Write first, edit second.

Most of us cannot hold very many thoughts or ideas in our head at once. Our thoughts are ill-formed and nebulous. When we write these thoughts down, though, we give them shape. We make it easier to see how they fit together, to find holes and problems, and to move the pieces around.

"Think it through, then write" is a mistake because writing is itself a process of thinking. Artists determine what the painting will look like as they paint. Musicians work out their solos as they play. Sculptors determine the shape as they chip away stone. Each artist starts with a basic idea, but it comes to life as the artist *produces* it. So it goes with writing. You learn what you're really trying to say by saying it.

This point may not be obvious unless you're already accustomed to doing it—to using writing as a process of thinking. Fear of path dependency is a pervasive phenomenon. Next time you sit down to write and feel stuck, ask yourself what's going on. You are probably not sure what to say and can't write anything until you figure it out. There you go. Write something down (including half-baked and contradictory ideas). Trust yourself to fix it—or delete it—later.

Writing and editing are separate processes. Writing is the way you figure stuff out; editing is the way you polish it. First, just write a bunch of stuff. Most of it will be bad. But then trust yourself to come back and delete the bad stuff. Extract the good ideas and work those into longer papers. Be willing to step away from your work and come back to it fresh. It'll be easier to see what's good and what's bad. Be willing to delete 80% of what you write.

An anecdote illustrating these ideas: I wrote a paper criticizing Julia Driver's theory of virtue in her excellent book *Uneasy Virtue*. I presented the paper at Dartmouth, where she worked at the time. She had good responses to my critique. I went home and deleted about twenty-nine and a half out of thirty manuscript pages. I took the one paragraph that had a good idea worth expanding upon and turned that into an entirely new thirty-page paper. That became my first paper accepted at a top-tier journal.

If you have good time management skills, you'll always have plenty of time to edit. You won't have to worry that you need to get eight thousand words out by tomorrow and so be stuck knowing that every word you write must be right and in the right place.

Once You Have a Hammer, Look for More Nails

Once you start producing new research full time, reading often feels like a luxury. Becoming an expert on a new topic consumes tremendous amounts of time.

One way to multiply your productivity is to ensure that after you've learned a field or acquired significant background knowledge, you can get multiple papers and projects out of it. For instance, I learned a great deal about voter psychology, voter ignorance, the pathologies of political behavior, and economic theories about the effects of voting. I used that to do a project on the individual ethics of voting, a different project on whether compulsory voting is a good idea, and a third project on the foundations of democracy itself.

Another way to multiply your productivity is to reuse the same argument, principle, or theory for new purposes. To illustrate, back in 2012, I published a paper that offered a refutation of what I called "symbolic or expressive arguments for democracy."[10] A few years later, I realized that my challenge to symbolic arguments for democracy also worked as a challenge to the symbolic/expressive/semiotic arguments various theorists have offered against kidney markets and other taboo markets.[11] Because the argument I developed in that 2012 paper can be used against pretty much any symbolic/expressive/semiotic argument anyone makes for or against any policy, I now keep that argument in my pocket, and I'm ready to pull it out to produce a new paper on a new topic.

The danger of this approach is that you want to avoid simply writing the same paper or book over and over. Using one theory or intellectual tool to accomplish six different tasks is great. Writing the exact same theory in six different forms is not, though some people get away with it.

Always Have Multiple Projects at Different Stages

Good work often takes years to develop. You have an idea. You write something. You get stuck on a puzzle, or your paper gets stuck in an unpublishable form. You need time not just to revise it but to step away so that you can view it later with fresh eyes. Sometimes you can't quite see where the book goes wrong, or what the real insight is in a paper, unless you've been alienated from the project for months or even years. Further, fatigue often sets in. You know the paper needs work, but you're bored. You want to work on something new.

There's no inherent problem with stepping away from a project for a while. Indeed, it's a good idea. (It's also a good idea to reread your old work from years ago, to see if there's something you missed and could expand.) The danger is that if you're only writing one paper at a time, then spending a few months off means getting nothing done.

To be productive, think of your research as being on a conveyer belt. Different things are at different stages. As one piece moves forward, the other pieces move with it, and something new gets placed at the beginning of the belt. The stages of the belt:

1 *Nascent ideas.* These are ideas for projects you want to work on in a few years. Though you aren't actively writing them, you've at least written down a list of questions and basic arguments, an outline of some possible experiments, or a description for the kind of data and test you'll need. When you read other things, you think about how these might help these projects. You talk these ideas over with colleagues and friends. You keep an eye out for readings related to them.

2 *Early drafts.* Papers you've just begun working on. You're following the "write first, edit later" method

here. Much of what you write is garbage, but you're planning to cut out the bad stuff and keep the good. You start sharing these things with colleagues.

3 *Polished drafts.* Working papers and chapters that look good. You put these up on websites for general comments. You present them at various conferences and at other universities.

4 *Papers under review.* Papers that are good enough to send out to peer-reviewed journals. You have at least three such papers under review at all times.

5 *Papers in press.* Papers that have been accepted and are in the process of proofing and copyediting.

6 *Published work.* It's in the journal. The book's in your hand. You aren't necessarily finished with it, however: you can promote it by sending copies to other academics or seeing if journalists and popular newspapers might cover it.

You might work on one project for a week or two at a time, but then need a break. That's not only acceptable, but recommended. The important thing is to not turn the break from the paper into a break from research, period. Instead, move on to a different paper and work on that for a while. Move things up the conveyer belt.

It helps to keep a spreadsheet or Word document listing what you're working on, what stage you've reached, and what you think needs to be done next. Refer to it from time to time. Even something as simple as keeping separate folders on your PC for projects in progress, projects under review, and finished projects helps.

For instance, as I write the first draft of this chapter, I'm waiting for my coauthors in two separate book projects and two separate articles to write their portions and to edit what I've written for those works. Once they hand me the manuscripts back, I'll take a break from this chapter and work on those things for a while. Once I've gone through them, I'll come back and edit this paragraph. Maybe I'll even delete it. (Guess not.)

Journal versus Book Publishing

Even for predominantly teaching-oriented positions, getting a job and earning tenure requires that you publish in whatever your field and your school considers "good outlets." In almost all fields, this means publishing *original* journal articles or books. In some fields, only articles count; in others, original books beat journal articles.

Textbooks or books meant for teaching purposes, encyclopedia articles, reference pieces, op-eds, book reviews, blogposts, medium.com diatribes, and the like either don't count or count for very little. One hundred book reviews won't get you tenure, but ten articles in *American Economic Review* will make you a full professor in pretty much any economics department.

In some parts of the humanities, scholars have been arguing that digital publications, blogging, and so on should replace the traditional journal or printed book model. They think alternative venues should count toward tenure. Again, remember that I am taking no stance here about how academia *ought* to be. My goal is to tell you what it takes to succeed given how things are.

Journal publishing is straightforward, in a way. You write a paper and submit it through an online submission form. It's largely anonymous. You should get a sense of what different journals publish. You don't want to waste time sending the wrong kind of work to a journal. Other than that, you just do your best work and send it to the best journals it fits. Then you wait and hope—and while you wait, you write something else.

Book publishing is a different story. Books go through extensive peer review, and getting a book published is extremely difficult (as is publishing in the very top journals). But unlike journal publications, book refereeing is not double-blind. You don't know who the referees are, but they know who you are. The reason for this is that it is tremendously expensive to publish a book. The publisher incurs significant financial risk. Academic presses aren't necessarily trying to turn a profit on each book—some books subsidize the others, and some universities subsidize their presses—but they can't lose too much money.

For this reason, book publishing involves a kind of Catch-22. Book publishers want to sign authors worthy of having their work published in book form, and the best way for them to know if you are such a person is for you to have already published a book. This means that once you've published a book with a good press, it's much easier to get the next book. You've shown whether you get a readership, can sell a few copies, and make a splash. You've also been vouched for. It's getting that first book that's tricky.

The editors at the good academic presses get dozens of "Might you be interested in reading my manuscript?" emails a week. A senior editor at a top academic press told me his acceptance rate for "unsolicited inquiries" was less than 1%. So, how do you overcome the odds and break in? Unfortunately, there's no easy strategy. But the following pointers will help:

1 Get hired in the top program in your field, or come from a top program. This sends a strong signal that you're an up-and-coming star. Publishers are looking for the next big thing.

2 Publish a few papers in the very top journals on a given topic. You can then approach an editor and explain how

you want to use these as the backbone of a book, though the book should include at least seventy percentage points worth of new material. That you were able to publish in a top journal is strong evidence you've got something worthwhile, something people will read.

3 Have an elite person in your field vouch for you and talk you up. I don't want to overstate how much this helps: so many professors do this nowadays that it may backfire. Still, the biggest problem with this strategy is that every advisor out there is trying to solicit book contracts for her star students, if not all her students, so it's much better if the person vouching for you has no personal stake in you. Some book publishers institutionalize the process of external pre-vetting by creating book series edited by an elite professor, who in turn goes looking for and vouches for new talent. (But getting noticed by that professor is then like getting noticed by a book editor directly.)

4 Get noticed by an editor and have her come to you. Of course, you can't just decide this will happen, but you can do things that make it more likely. You can follow strategies 1 or 2, and then editors might come knocking. You can also increase your public presence. Get a paper published in a good journal, but then turn that paper into op-eds, magazine interviews, podcasts and radio interviews, and so on. If you can show that you can both (a) publish serious academic research at a high level and (b) get that research profiled and discussed among the lay public, then you're a good bet.

Dealing with Email

Success in academia is all about time management. Good time management means doing the *important* stuff first, when you have the most brainpower and willpower. Leave the urgent but unimportant stuff until the end of the day.

You might get a hundred emails a day when you are midcareer. If you answer email first thing in the morning, you might well spend many hours just on email. Email has a tendency to consume as many hours as you give it. Happily, however, answering emails can be compressed into a short amount of time. Maybe you give yourself twenty-five minutes at the end of each workday to answer emails. If you write short but polite responses, you can get much of it done.

Keep in mind that not every email needs a response. For instance, the day after you submit grades, you might get ten emails of the form "I'm disappointed in my grade and wonder if you would reconsider it." By all means, if the student has a real argument or provides evidence that you made a real error, reconsider it. But many students do this to all their professors as a matter of routine, thinking it can't hurt to pressure them for a better grade. You don't need to respond to each student by explaining your grading policy. You could instead just delete the emails and move on.

Keep in mind also that many emails require a no. And that brings me to my next point.

Learn to Say No, Especially to Service Work

Remember that you have a time budget. An hour spent on one thing is an hour not spent on another. You have to spend your time wisely, and you won't be able to "buy" everything worth doing because some things exceed your budget.

You may receive multiple speaking invitations every week. Any professor with a research profile might be asked to contribute a paper to an anthology or a special issue of a journal.

You might be asked to attend a workshop, do a guest lecture, or take on an additional class offload. Since service is part of your job, you may be asked to chair or participate in a committee, help with admissions, participate in some alumni or donor event, oversee a case competition, coach or tutor students preparing for certain academically oriented extracurriculars, or any number of thousands of other activities, mundane or profound. Outside of the university, you'll be asked to referee papers and grant proposals, allow high school students to interview you, answer queries from reporters, and more.

In isolation, many of these things are valuable, while some are in themselves a waste of time. Nevertheless, you have to advocate for yourself and learn to decline requests, politely.

Requests for your service time can be especially bad if you are a woman or a minority faculty member. Universities lament that white males are overrepresented in most fields. To prove their commitment to diversity and ensure that minority voices influence policy, they may ask for far too much service from female or minority faculty. The fewer the minorities on the faculty, the more administrators may pester such faculty for service work. Learn to say no. Don't let them use you.

Keep in mind that administrators often have completely different incentives from yours. As Benjamin Ginsberg explains in his excellent book *The Fall of the Faculty*, faculty (especially research faculty) are largely judged on output. My raise depends on what I publish, not on how much I work. In contrast, administrators often perform duties with invisible or hard to measure outputs. To demonstrate they deserve their paychecks, they often want to be seen as being as busy as possible. They have financial incentives to increase the amount of their committee work and the length and number of meetings they attend.[12] Since their bosses can't easily measure administrators' outputs, their bosses judge them by their inputs. Watch out.

Academics often tell themselves they can't say no. They imagine they will suffer all sorts of negative consequences or harms if they do. They're bad at standing up for themselves. In reality, if you say no politely, that's usually the end of it.

For assistant professors in Georgetown's business school, research is officially 60% of the job, teaching 30%, and service 10%, at least when it comes to assessing merit raises. The reality is that when it comes to promotion to associate professor, research is more likely worth 90% and the other two areas not much at all.

These kinds of numbers tell faculty how they ought to behave. If service is *really* worth only 5% of the job, then you should be spending no more than 5% of your time on service. If they ask for more, you say, "Thanks, but I'm already doing A, B, and C. That's my fair share."

Your school values what it rewards. If a liberal arts college says it values service and teaching but in fact attaches raises to research, then what it really values is research. The administrators may not be lying, but what they're saying is still false. If a school says it values teaching but gives the good offices and the summer bonuses to the people who raise grant money, then that's what it values.

If your school wants you to do something but doesn't pay you or reward you for it—and instead punishes you for doing it—then your school is trying to exploit you. Don't let it. In the end, remember that no one is going to advocate for you if you don't advocate for yourself. You should do your job and do it well. That doesn't mean making yourself into a doormat for others to walk on or a tool for others to use.

Principles for Efficient, Effective Teaching

The typical professor teaches six classes a year, three classes per semester. Sometimes these are multiple sections of the same course, and sometimes these can be six distinct classes. A professor in, say, political science might teach three sections of Introduction to Political Science, one section of Introduction to Political Theory, and then two higher-level, more specialized classes. Perhaps every few years she can teach a class corresponding to her research specialties or dissertation topic, but in general, she'll teach the basic courses students need for general education requirements and to complete the political science major.

Six classes a year equals about 270 contact hours in the classroom. (An average semester-long course meets for 45 hours per semester.) This doesn't include any time spent preparing the class, such as creating PowerPoint slides, writing exams, reading the assigned materials, or writing out lectures. In addition, professors must hold two to three open office hours per week. During exam weeks or when papers are due, students will email and request more time. After exams or papers are in, most professors must spend many hours grading.

It's hard to find good data on the average college class size in the United States, though the overwhelming majority of classes have fewer than fifty students.[13] Let's say a professor has six classes of thirty-five students each over the year, and each class has five major assignments (three papers and two tests). If the professor were to spend one hour grading each of those assignments, he'd spend over a thousand hours a year grading.

Even though most professors are teachers first and researchers second or third, this kind of practice is unsustainable. To avoid burning out and working overly long hours, professors need to find ways to be effective in the classroom without spending fifteen hundred or more hours a year on teaching-related work.

Here, then, are some suggestions toward that end.

1 *Use others' syllabi and course materials.* The average pizza shop needn't invent a recipe from scratch. Neither must you. For almost any course you might teach, hundreds or even thousands of other professors have already taught that course. They've tested different methods of instruction and different assignments. Many of them have already posted their syllabi and notes about teaching online, on their personal webpages. Others will gladly send you copies of their syllabi if you email them and ask. The first time you teach a course, a quick Google search for others' course materials, slides, and so on may save you hours. You don't need to copy others' syllabi exactly, of course. You can mix and match sections of different courses and customize them to your own ends.

2 *Grade less.* Many faculty grade too much. They write extensive comments on each section of each student's paper. They circle spelling and grammatical errors. They write a page of comments for every two pages of a student's paper. They require students to turn in problem sets and then grade each problem set. (Do you really need to do that in a college course? Why not assign homework but leave it to students to decide whether to actually do it?)

Instead of writing two pages of detailed comments that students will have difficulty parsing, just tell them one, two, or three big things they need to fix or change. (Ask yourself: When you get referee comments, do you benefit more from six paragraphs of detailed nitpicking or from two to three short but big comments?) Don't circle every spelling or grammatical error; just tell them they need to proofread better. Advise them to go to your university's writing center before passing in the next paper.

One way to grade less is to use *peer grading*. Instead of grading problem sets yourself, have students randomly redistribute the problem sets in class, and then have them grade them with answer keys you provide. You can have students place their student IDs instead of their names on the papers to preserve anonymity. You might require every student to bring a first draft of a paper to class, and then spend a class period having their peers read the papers and offer comments and criticisms.

3 *Prep Less.* Remember that the labor theory of value is false. You don't become a better teacher by writing out each lecture as if it were a paper. You don't improve student learning by making every PowerPoint slide immaculate and beautiful. If you're going to lecture, you should know the material well enough to do it off the cuff. The point of prepping is to organize your thoughts about what to cover and when. It's to help you think of intriguing ways to convey the material.

4 *Try lecturing less.* Instead of delivering a long lecture, is there a game or some sort of learning activity students can do that illustrates the central concept you wish to teach that day? You can send students away from the classroom for half an hour, have them perform some action, and then report back with their results. Can you have them do some version of a psychological or sociological experiment in class? Perhaps you might

even do the experiment *on them*, for their own erudition. Is there a simulation activity? Is there a short film or documentary you can have students watch and discuss?

I'm not advocating lazy teaching here. I think if you take a job you should do it well. Rather, my point is that for many topics, there are alternative ways of teaching the material that are as effective (or more effective) than lecturing and that take less time. See if you can discover or invent such methods—or inherit them from others.

5 *Have the students lead the class.* Consider assigning students to be discussion leaders in class. Each day, two new students are tasked with delivering a short lecture on that day's readings. They then distribute a set of questions—or provide an activity—to the other students. You pitch in to help. You walk around, listen in, and help correct any mistakes you hear.

6 *Read teaching journals.* Many academic fields maintain journals dedicated to teaching: for example, the *Journal of Business Ethics Education*, *Teaching Philosophy*, the *Journal of Economics Teaching*, and *Sociology Teaching*. Take a few hours each summer to scan through these for in-class activities, new kinds of assignments, and teaching methods. You may learn that there are far more effective and less labor-intensive methods of delivering a good education.

7 *Copy what works.* With some effort, you can discover who the successful teachers are at your college, or near you. Ask them if you can sit in on their classes. Offer to buy them lunch and then pick their brains about how to teach. Ask if you can have and use their teaching materials. Most will be flattered that you asked. Find out what works, and then do it too. You don't need to

invent your teaching methods from scratch through repeated trial and error. You can stand on the shoulders of those who came before you. Indeed, you owe it to your students (and perhaps yourself) to do so, to start off strong.

If You Don't Enjoy It, Change It or Quit

Academic success isn't worthwhile success if it's not making you happy. Unless you're at the very top of the academic salary distribution, you can probably earn as much or more money in an equally high-status job outside academia. You can probably find some other job that is spiritually and intellectually rewarding. Remember that you are a volunteer, not a conscript.

The job should be rewarding. You've got to enjoy raising students up a little, seeing their eyes light up when they suddenly "get it," hearing the insightful comment or question, and knowing that you're helping them achieve their goals. You've got to enjoy reading new insights or rediscovering old ones in academic texts. You have to wake up hungry to write down the ideas in your head. Otherwise, do yourself a favor and move on.

- There is always more worthwhile work to do, so having a good work/life balance means learning to turn down worthwhile research, teaching, and service endeavors.
- You may feel that academia is a calling, but you have the right to treat it like a job. You may need to do so to avoid burning out.
- Remember that work has diminishing marginal benefits and increasing marginal costs. Determine a time budget based on MB = MC. Stick to it.
- Being busy is beside the point. The goal is to be productive, not busy.
- You can succeed in academia and have a happy home life. It means spending your most productive hours on whatever is most important for your job, spending the remaining time on whatever's left, and saying no to many requests.
- With good time management and the word *no*, you can work forty hours a week most weeks.
- Don't let the urgent take precedence over the important. For many professors and for all grad students, that means don't let email or teaching get in the way of research productivity.
- Earn rewards, then take them.
- There are many strategies for picking exciting research topics. Try to write things that people outside your narrow subfield could care about and that people a century from now will still want to read.
- Write first, read second. Present partially finished papers to others. They'll help you debug your work.
- Writing is thinking. Writer's block comes from a fear of getting stuck with bad ideas. Learn to figure things out as you write, then go back and edit the material into something usable. The most important key on the keyboard is *Delete*.
- There are many strategies for getting good teaching results with less work, including asking for others' teaching materials and substituting activities for lectures.
- Once you learn a literature, try to get multiple papers out of it. Once you develop a theory or an argument, try to use it for multiple purposes.
- Always have different projects at different stages. When you get tired or bored or stuck on one thing, switch to another.

- Book publishing is harder to break into than journal publishing, in part because it does not make use of double-blind review. Editors tend to reject unsolicited manuscript proposals.
- What your deans reward—via salary raises and promotions—is what they value. If they don't count service for much in tenure and promotion decisions, then you have every right to advocate for yourself by saying no to service projects. If they treat service as 10% of your job, you don't owe them more than two hundred hours of service a year, if even that.
- You are a volunteer, not a conscript. If you don't enjoy the work, make a change or quit.

FOUR

The Academic Market and Tenure

Going on the Market

Academic work is good work if you can get it, but you have to get it.

As we discussed in chapter 1, the basic "who gets it" numbers are lousy. On average, only about half of new PhD students eventually get a PhD. Slightly more than one in five first-year PhD students eventually obtains a long-term faculty job. Slightly more than one in ten obtains a tenure-track job. According to the *Chronicle of Higher Education*'s 2015 "Almanac" issue, only 31.8% of all PhD students have definite employment plans upon graduation. Of those with definite employment plans, slightly more than half have firm academic plans.[1]

Those are the raw numbers. But remember to avoid the Go Pro fallacy. These aren't exactly the odds for you, given the additional information you have about yourself. If you're a fourth-year PhD student in MIT's economics department with three papers already published in the *American Economic Review* and the *Journal of Political Economy*, your chances of landing a tenure-track research job in a top-twenty department might be around 95%. If you're a first-year English PhD student at the 125th-ranked department, and you're not working toward publishing, your odds of getting a tenure-track job might be near 0%.

The odds are partly up to you because what your CV looks like when you hit the market is partly up to you. How you do, however, is not entirely up to you. Maybe journal referees will consistently be unfair to you, despite your best efforts. Maybe hiring committees are bored by your research topic, and you couldn't have predicted that. Maybe this year there are no jobs in your specialty, though there were fifteen openings last year.

So it goes. Nevertheless, it's dangerous to decry how your success depends on others' decisions. In general, people who have or develop an internal locus of control instead spend their time working to improve their odds and, as a result, end up having better odds.[2] In the academic job market, everyone who succeeds is lucky, but few are *merely* lucky. The people who get jobs, especially the plum jobs, may not always be the most deserving, but they are almost always deserving.

The academic job market is not a lottery: who gets a job and who doesn't is not random chance. In most fields, it's a buyer's market, which means that employers have both the power and the incentive to pick excellent people. Hiring committees—the "buyers"—get applications from hundreds of candidates who do everything to demonstrate their excellence. They'll rarely pick *bad* candidates.

The previous chapters focused on success in graduate school and on life as an academic teacher and researcher more generally. This chapter concerns going on the market, going up for tenure, and what to do if academia doesn't work out.

The Basics of the Market

When it comes to hiring faculty, most academic fields follow the same pattern. First, in the late summer or early fall, departments advertise their tenure-track job openings for the next academic year. For instance, political science departments will advertise in summer through early fall 2020 for jobs that begin in fall 2021.

In most fields, there is a centralized place where most, if not all, of the jobs are advertised. In philosophy, it's philjobs.org. In economics, it's https://www.aeaweb.org/joe/listings. In political science, it's https://www.apsanet.org/eJobs. And so on. Your advisors and other graduate students can tell you where to look. Some schools also publish jobs at chroniclevitae.com or other websites.

Job advertisements usually say what subfield the job is for (e.g., political theory). They might specify a preferred research area (e.g., immigration and nationality), the range of courses the successful applicant must teach, the normal teaching load at the university, and they might mention something generic but noncommittal about salary ("highly competitive" or "contingent upon qualifications"). They'll tell you how to apply and what to include in your dossier.

You should apply for every job you might be qualified for, even if you don't meet all listed requirements or have quite the preferred research focus. Job descriptions are sometimes more like "wish lists" than sets of necessary conditions or genuine requirements. East Nowhere State may advertise for people with six publications in seventeenth-century Albanian cultural history, but in reality they'll hire someone working on general European history.

At any rate, the marginal cost to you of applying for one extra job is often only about five or ten minutes of work. You revise a cover letter slightly and submit things through one more website. No one will punish you for applying for a job you don't quite fit. So, apply for everything relevant. Let *them* say no. (As a person on the other side, I hope you don't follow my advice here; nevertheless, you should follow it.)

I repeat: You should apply for every job for which you might be qualified. There's another reason why. Unless you're that rock-star MIT econ student I mentioned above, you can't afford to be selective. Some grad students think, "I'll only apply for low teaching load tenure-track jobs at these seven elite universities in my three favorite cities." That's a recipe for unemployment. You can afford to be picky when and if you receive multiple offers. Picky is for people with options. In most fields, there are too many excellent candidates for you to be selective about where you apply.

Instead, use this selection mechanism: For every advertised job, if you would prefer (a) taking that job to (b) quitting academia forever, then apply.

The departments will each screen hundreds of applications. Some will ask a few candidates, perhaps as many as fifty or as few as twenty, for further information, writing samples, and the like. Some departments ask every candidate to send a full dossier. Others ask candidates to send only a cover letter and CV at first; they then ask a minority to send a full dossier.

Next, departments make a "long list" of ten to fifteen candidates for "first round" interviews. In the past, departments would usually conduct these hour-long interviews at the field's annual academic conference, such as the American Philosophical Association's Eastern Division meeting or the Academy of Management's conference. Today, many departments instead do first-round interviews by Skype.

There's a considerable academic literature showing that job interviews are worse than useless. They reinforce biases and are largely unreliable guides to candidate quality.[3] Nevertheless, most academic departments persist in using them.

Departments then select three to five of these candidates for second-round, on-campus interviews. During on-campus interviews, candidates usually present one of their working papers or a recent publication in a seminar. They may perform a teaching demonstration or deliver a guest lecture in a class. They eat a few fancy meals with the faculty. They meet one-on-one, for an hour at a time, with each professor in the hiring department. They might also meet separately with some undergrad or graduate students.

When you interview on campus, you'll meet with a dean, provost, or some other senior administrator. If you get an offer, one of them will be the official person making the offer. At both points, you can and should ask what it takes to get tenure. Ask for *numbers*: five A-level journal articles? What counts as A-level? If you get an offer, ask for written answers to your questions.

Finally, the committee will rank the candidates from the on-campus interviews. The #1 candidate will be offered the job first. If she declines, they'll move on to the #2 candidate. And so on. If all the on-campus interviewees decline (because they received better offers elsewhere), they might bring out a few more long-list candidates, they might cancel the search, or they might hold off and repeat the search again a year later.

While first-round interviews kind of stink, on-campus interviews are almost fun. During on-campus interviews, the dynamics change slightly. Once someone brings you to campus, they're already convinced you're smart. Now they're trying to decide whether they want you or someone else to be around. You aren't trying to prove you've got the basic chops as much as showing that you would be a good colleague.

Further, departments don't want their offers to be declined. It hurts their feelings to some degree. ("Thanks, Penn, but I'd rather work at Princeton.") Worse, their deans may *punish* them if the offers are turned down. If too many offers are declined, the dean or provost might chastise the department for ineffective recruitment and, in some cases, even cancel the search, costing the department a potential colleague. For this reason, on-campus interviews are more of a mutual kicking of the tires. The faculty and dean will try to *sell* the department and the college to you. They'll try to convince you that it's a great place to live and work.

Toward the end of the yearly job cycle, when the tenure-track job searches are in their final stages, departments begin advertising non-tenure-track long-term jobs (such as teaching professorships, lecturer gigs, and so on) and temporary jobs (postdocs, visiting assistant professorships). In most fields, come February, applicants know they've failed to get a tenure-track job, so they're open to accepting these alternative, less desirable jobs.

In any given year, a few departments will be granted the right to hire tenure-track professors and will advertise quite late in the year. So, wherever your field advertises jobs, keep looking. A great tenure-track gig meant to start August 1 might appear out of nowhere on May 1. Because the advertisement for that job appears so late, the competition will be less, and the job will be easier to get.

The Dossier: Everything Must Have a Hook

Remember: Even the crummiest full-time academic jobs receive hundreds of applications. In some fields, especially for weird job openings that span multiple disciplines, the applications can number in the thousands.

I mentioned before that when I'm on hiring committees, the typical (in the technical sense of *modal*) amount of time I spend reading each application is about twenty seconds. Some faculty spend more like four minutes. But no one spends an hour per application. There isn't enough time for that. Most applications get discarded quickly. Only a minority receive close scrutiny.

It is, therefore, crucial that your dossier hook readers in. That can be hard to do, because the dossier is so large. A dossier will typically include a CV, a letter of interest, a research summary, a teaching summary, a writing sample, recommendation letters, and evidence of teaching effectiveness. It may consist of seven or more documents totaling more than one hundred pages.

Different faculty may look at different things first. I always start with the CV, looking at (1) PhD institution, (2) previous academic positions, and (3) publications. At the Harris School at the University of Chicago, they read the abstracts of everyone's writing sample as an initial screening mechanism.[4] Some start with your cover letter. Others go straight to recommendation letters. Regardless, most of the time, they're not going to read your entire application.

What this means for you is that the first page of every document you include in your dossier must have a hook. You must grip the reader. You should assume that whoever is reading your application will read the first paragraph of any document at random and, if not immediately intrigued and impressed, will throw the whole thing out. Page 1 of your writing sample has to sell the paper. Page 1 of your CV has to sell the rest.[5]

Your writing sample can't begin with three pages of boring literature review. You mustn't hide your intriguing thesis and central argument on page 6 or reveal that fascinating puzzle you'll solve on page 8. It has to go on page 1. Page 1 is usually all you get.

Page 1 of your CV needs to display your most impressive achievement. Whatever the best reason is to give you the job goes up front. If you won a national teaching award, received a giant grant, or published a book as a third-year grad student, say so right away. Write like a journalist—put the big things up front and the fine details in the back.

Don't Be Boring

A grad student in another program once wrote asking me to critique his research statement/summary. He had heard me speak about how most research statements are boring. He asked me to be blunt and honest. I told him, more gently than I'm stating it here, something like this: "There are maybe twenty people in the entire world who care about this topic. I am one of them. Yet after reading your research statement, even I don't want to know more."

I wasn't suggesting he throw out his dissertation or change to a new topic. I wasn't saying his research was bad, derivative, or uninteresting. His dissertation was great; probably better than mine, really. The problem was how he presented the work. I suggested that he rewrite his abstract. The goal: Try to explain your research in a way that's so interesting that your hairdresser would want to read it.

He took my advice, rewrote the statement from scratch a few times, and made his in-fact intriguing research *sound* intriguing. He got the postdoc and then later obtained a good tenure-track job. Now, maybe he would have succeeded anyway. Or maybe he succeeded because he learned how to *sell* his research.

Most academics don't learn how to sell what they do. If you haven't, I'm not blaming you. You may simply be copying how others in the field write. Most academics are boring, flat writers. To be clear: They succeeded despite their bad writing, not because of it.

In part, academics are boring because of the dynamics of education. Your high school, undergraduate, and graduate professors may have offered you advice about being a better writer. They may have demanded you submit multiple drafts and rewrite papers. Nevertheless, there's always a problem: your teachers and professors were paid to read your work. They generally read all of it.

In the real world, though, including academia, people aren't getting paid to read your work, even when they're getting paid to read *some* work. Your research is competing with *Game of Thrones*, drinking craft beer, playing tennis, taking a nap, prepping classes, chatting with co-workers, revising the reader's own research, and reading all the other research out there. You must work hard to induce people to start reading your work and then work hard to keep them reading after two pages.

Remember: The first page of your research statement may be all the typical hiring committee member plans to read, unless you convince her otherwise. Further, the hiring committee member reading your application may have just read fifty applications in a row before she looks at yours. She's bored and annoyed. Her eyes are starting to glaze over. The good news, though, is that most of your competitors write boring applications, even though they do excellent work. If you stand out—if you make readers think, "Wow, I'd like to know *more*"— then you might just get the job.

Here are three good practical tips for making your writing better.

1 Some word processors, such as Word, can estimate the reading level of your work. Aim for a twelfth-grade reading level or lower.

2 Cut fifty words from each page of your writing sample.

3 Read every paper out loud. If it doesn't flow, rewrite it.

These tips won't make you come across as less sophisticated. On the contrary, anyone with a thesaurus can write in a convoluted, ornate way. Anyone can hide a half-baked idea behind vague, opaque prose that creates the illusion of profundity. To be able to explain a profound and complicated idea—say, quantum mechanics—in plain and simple English requires genuine talent. You can't fake that around experts. It proves you're smart. It makes you a more desirable candidate. It's also *some* evidence you can teach well.

Further, forcing yourself to write in simple language often reveals to you where the gaps in your argument are. Sometimes your argument only seems airtight because even you don't understand what you really mean.

Tortured writing is easy. Writing that seems effortless takes real skill.

Your CV Tells a Story

I was once on the yearly hiring committee for a prestigious postdoc program. I remember reading the "presentations" section of the CV of an Ivy League applicant. The first year, the student presented at the annual graduate workshop in his department. The next year, he branched out to the regional political science association and did a talk at a neighboring university. Then, for the next three years, he presented only at the graduate workshop at his own school. He had no publications.

Ask: What story does that CV tell? First, the applicant practices by doing a local presentation. Good. Then he branches out to regional conference and gives a real talk at a neighbor's. Great. Sounds like he's professionalizing. But for the next three years he only presents at the graduate workshop his own department runs for its students. Story: He stopped professionalizing. He dipped his toes in the waters but didn't swim. He retreated into the warm comfort of home. Our reaction: Rejection.

We also saw many CVs where applicants had conducted dozens of professional presentations but never published anything. The story: These applicants are starters, but not finishers. Reaction: Rejection.

When you go up for tenure, your CV will tell a story. Suppose an external referee examines your profile. She sees that for the first three years of your career, you have no publications. Then, in years four and five, you finally get two hits. In your tenure application, you say you have three more papers under review. You mention that you are "shopping" your dissertation to different presses. The story: This person plans to publish the bare minimum to get tenure, and then never publish again. Reaction: A negative letter advising your president not to give you tenure.

Here are some other stories you don't want your CV to tell:

1 My work consists primarily of applying my advisor's ideas to new things. I'm like the light beer or discount version of my advisor. You can get half my advisor for half the price!
2 I plan on republishing my dissertation as many times as I can until I get tenure. Six years into being a professor, I'll only be working on extracts from my dissertation. I'm never going to move on to something new. I'm a one-hit wonder—if I even manage to have a hit.

3 I'm a liar. I have no publications, but I have a "Publica-tions and Presentations" section of my CV, where I list only presentations and papers *under review*. I'm hoping this will trick you into taking a closer look at me. (In-stead: If you have no papers published or accepted for publication, then the word *publication* shouldn't appear on your CV. In the same way, unlike some engineering professors, I have no patents, so the word *patent* doesn't appear on my CV.)

4 I'm a liar. I'm going to try to pass off these book reviews or short two-page reply articles as if they were full-length original articles. I hope you don't notice.

5 Despite completing six years of grad school and a two-year postdoc, I think my undergraduate awards and GPA are a good reason to hire me.

6 I don't understand what academia is. I spent my time in grad school not publishing papers or learning to teach, but instead on graduate student government and political activism. If you hire me, I'll annoy the deans, induce alumni to write angry letters, and make sure faculty meetings go on and on. I won't focus on the actual job—you know, teaching and publishing.

7 I volunteered for every service activity I could as a grad student, but didn't publish anything. I'll relieve the rest of you of committee work for six years, but then I won't get tenure, because I didn't publish.

You want your CV to tell a much different story:

1 I am an original thinker.
2 I can contribute something new to existing conversations.
3 I can also start new conversations.
4 I can do the job better than anyone else you can hire.

5 Even after getting tenure, I'll never stop publishing. I will publish more than you expect I should do.

6 I will rock my classes. People will major in our subject just to take class with me. Hiring me means more money for the department.

7 I'll be a good citizen. I'll be fun to have around. You'll want to go to lunch with me.

8 I understand how academia works, and I prioritize what's actually the priority.

Practice Your Pitch(es)

When I was a graduate student, my advisor (Dave) had his students meet for lunch every other week. We'd discuss where we were in our studies and where we planned to be for the next meeting. We discussed why we made progress and what we could do if we hadn't. We talked strategies for productivity. We also just plain socialized.

We started each meeting the same way: every student writing a dissertation had to give a five-minute "pitch" about his dissertation. Dave's students practiced both five-minute first-round-interview-style pitches and a one-minute "elevator" pitch. The five-minute pitch is for the "Tell us about your dissertation" question one gets during a first-round interview. The one-minute pitch is for networking.

Memorize your pitch. It should roll out of you effortlessly. You need to be able to deliver it perfectly even when you're stressed and tired.

A good pitch should immediately spark the listeners' interest. Perhaps it starts by saying, "Everyone thinks X but here's why X can't be right." Perhaps it presents a puzzle: "How can both A and B be true?" Perhaps it deals with some gripping current event. "Z happens all the time, but no one has a good theory of Z." Or perhaps it solves an unsolved mystery. "Anthropologists have long wondered why X. My dissertation explains why."

A good pitch should present a clear and identifiable thesis, argument, and methodology. It should skip the "lit review" and get right to the point. "Here's my conclusion. Here's my central argument for that conclusion. Here's the kind of data I use or method I use to demonstrate my thesis. Here's why that matters."

A good pitch, like a good research statement, is not written for your advisor, who cares about you. It's not written for you, a person who found your topic compelling enough to devote two to five years to writing about it. (Let's hope it was two, not five.) It shouldn't even be aimed at people in your field, exactly. Aim instead to say something so interesting that laypeople would want to hear more. But then simultaneously demonstrate to the experts that you have great technical sophistication.

Questions You Must Be Able to Answer

If you succeed in getting a few first-round or on-campus interviews, you can expect to answer the same questions over and over. Many questions are obvious and routine. Committees ask you about your dissertation. They present some objections or counterarguments. My advice here: Answer their objections thoroughly, but don't act as if their objections are stupid, even when they are. Make the questioners feel smart for asking and make yourself seem smart for answering.

They ask you about your teaching experience. They go over the stuff in your application. You're probably prepared for all that. No problem. But some questions are harder to answer. The reasons the committee asks them, or how to answer them, may be obscure. Here are some examples and how to handle them.

What kind of research do you anticipate doing five years from now? Ten? (Translation: What's next?)

The point of this question is to see if you have new ideas on the back burner. The committee wants to know you have multiple projects at different stages, all going down the conveyer belt. They want to know you have work submitted for review, work you're polishing, work you're starting, and also good ideas in the back of your mind that you'll pursue full time in the future. The hiring committee wants to know that you're the kind of person who will keep publishing new ideas for as long as you have a job. They want to know you are interested in more than one thing.

A great way to answer this question is to deliver a five-minute pitch for the book you haven't even started writing, or on the series of papers on a new research topic you haven't even begun. Though you aren't actively writing these things yet, you demonstrate you nevertheless have a compelling hypothesis and know how to test it. You know where and how to get the data you need. You know you won't get scooped and the issue will matter five years from now. You thereby show the committee that in the future, you'll keep producing new work.

A bad—but the most common—answer to this question is, "Oh, I plan to be getting the fifth article out of my dissertation and then trying to turn it into a book." Though it's not your intention, what you thereby express is, "I have one idea. I'm going to push that one idea as long as I can." You come across as the person who will do the bare minimum to get tenure, and then retire.

By the way, saying "I want to turn my dissertation into a book" is uninteresting. In book-oriented fields (English, philosophy, history, political theory), *everybody* says that. What's more interesting is if you can provide the committee with evidence that you will indeed *publish* a book or two in the next seven years. "I have a contract with Cambridge University Press to publish my dissertation as a book; it's due May 31 next year" is a great answer. No one expects a grad student to have a book contract with a good press, but if you do, you'll probably get a good job.

Tell me more about [random thing on your CV you think is unimportant]

I attended a professionalization seminar as a third-year grad student. We did mock interviews. Turns out I wasn't prepared. Political theorist John Tomasi asked me about a paper I'd presented at a conference, a paper I'd largely forgotten about. The paper wasn't in my area of specialty and was unrelated to my dissertation topic. I couldn't remember my central argument. Oops.

John gave me this advice: You must be ready to discuss anything on your CV for an hour. You don't know what interviewers will find interesting or why they're interviewing you. What this means is that you don't just need good pitches for your dissertation, your job market papers, and for the projects you plan to do five years from now. You also need a good pitch for every presentation, paper, or class mentioned on your CV.

Tomasi's advice saved me from blowing one interview. Though my dissertation was on meta-ethics, at one of my first-round interviews, the interviewers were a metaphysician, a philosopher of language, and a philosopher of science. They spent half an hour asking me about my one small publication in the philosophy of physics/metaphysics. That's what they knew, so that's what we talked about.

I recommend creating a cheat sheet for yourself. Write up a bullet-point list or study guide for everything on your CV. Read it between interviews.

A corollary of that last bit of advice: It would be helpful if your CV has so much good stuff on it you actually *need* a study sheet to help you remember how to pitch your work. If you have no publications, no presentations, and no teaching, you won't need this study guide, but you're less likely to get interviewed, period.

How would you teach, and would you be happy to teach [any random class the department offers]?

Regardless of whether you're interviewing at a twenty-five-person or three-person department, you should be prepared and willing to teach a wide range of courses within the department, not just classes in your narrow specialty. In the big department, people might take turns teaching the introductory "service" classes. Perhaps they always stick the junior people with them. In the small departments, four professors might have to cover twenty different courses. This means they need whomever they hire to be competent to teach five courses in any given year and ten long term.

They ask this question in part to determine whether you can fulfill their needs. The senior faculty members might well be hoping they can dump some class they dislike on you once you're hired. When they ask this question, they're also trying to determine how *broad* you are. Every candidate knows her subfield. They want to determine if you know your field in general.

At any rate, the best answer is, "Yes, I'm happy to teach that class. And, I just so happen to have brought with me a sample syllabus for that very class." Then you pull out four copies of a sample syllabus, with a great reading list and an innovative pedagogy. If you took my advice in chapter 2 about using your TA time effectively, then you can leave graduate school already prepared to teach any class in your specialty, your areas of competence, and areas in which you've assisted.

Why do you want to work here?

The most honest answer to this question, 90% of the time is: "I want a job. This is a job. If you make me an offer, it'll probably be the only offer I get. I'd be grateful to get something. It's either this or selling life insurance." The truth is that—unless you're a rock star likely to get multiple offers—the hiring committee already knows this is your most honest answer. They're not trying to trick you, but they're looking for more.

Can you say something good about the department? About the students or the school? Would you be happy to live there? Even though the college may be in the middle of nowhere, you can point out how you love fishing and hiking. Maybe your husband's parents live nearby, and that will make him happy. Maybe you grew up in Western New York, and you miss the lake-effect snow. Small things like that help.

Can you talk about what the other faculty do? Can you demonstrate why you'd be delighted to hang out with them and chat about their work? Could you show that even if this is just "a job," you'd nevertheless intrinsically enjoy being there? Maybe you have experience teaching students like theirs and can explain why you enjoy teaching such students.

Good answers to these questions signal that you've done your homework. They signal conscientiousness and time-management skills. They suggest you might well become a good citizen who'll invest in the department. They signal that you might well be someone happy to be there—and thus a joy to have around—rather than someone bitter because he didn't end up at Yale. They signal that you might stick around long term. The committee won't get stuck trying to replace you in three years after you leave for greener pastures. (Keep in mind that if departments have a hard time retaining junior faculty, deans might punish them by refusing to authorize replacement hires.)

Do you have any questions for us?

Interviewers always ask if you have any questions for them. It's almost a throwaway question, but you can use it to your advantage. This question tests whether you've done your homework and can demonstrate some level of conscientious engagement. "No questions" is a bad answer. Any question that could have been answered by reading their website—e.g., "How many undergrads are there at Syracuse?"—is a bad question.

A good response asks a question that shows you have real interest in the department or school. "Where do you see the department growing? How could someone like me best contribute to your long-term plans?" Or, "I see you have a Center for X. I happen to be interested in X, as the following stories illustrate. How can I get more involved?"

Here was my stock response to this question when I was on the job market. I used it maybe forty or so times and always got a good response: "Every department has a different culture. Let me ask you, then, what does it take to be a good colleague in your department?" Notice what this signals: I want to be a good colleague. I remember asking that question during a first-round interview at a Catholic university. The chair of the department, a Catholic priest, responded, "Son, that's a damn good question."

By the way, sometimes the way faculty answer this question will show you that you won't want that job, at least if you have multiple offers. During one of my interviews, a professor responded: "I think a good colleague is someone who reads my papers and offers constructive advice, but doesn't expect me to return the favor." Turns out he wasn't kidding. I asked around and discovered that the people in that department hate each other. A friend of mine accepted that job and hated it.

Why should your application be on top of the pile?

Being asked why your application should be on the top of the pile is a weird question. I've heard it more often at business schools than at liberal arts departments. But you might just get a question like this.

You can use it to reiterate your key strengths. You can argue that you're a sure bet—you'll do a great job and be around a long time. You might—and this is tricky—even know who the other applicants are, and you might use it to explain why you're a better bet than they are, without mentioning them explicitly.

At any rate, use this as another opportunity to sell yourself to the department. If the language of "selling yourself" offends you, feel free to use a less offensive synonym. But learn to sell yourself.

Do you have kids? How old are they? Are you married? Etc.

Questions like these are inappropriate and illegal. The interviewing departments' HR administrators warned your interviewers not to ask them. They either know better or should know better.

Alternatively, in some cases, such questions are harmless. Maybe you've already broached the issue—you told them you have kids—so they're trying to be helpful to you as potential future colleagues. Maybe they want to advertise the good local schools or the awesome local children's museum. Maybe they want you to know your spouse could easily find a job.

Regardless of whether such questions are legal or appropriate, you should prepare to deal with questions like these. A good response isn't, "How dare you ask? I'm reporting you to your HR department." Maybe they deserve that, but giving them what they deserve won't do you much good. A better response would be to avoid answering such questions in a way that also prevents them from feeling awkward or criticized, even if they deserve it. Maybe you could answer their question with a question. "Do you have any children?" "Thanks for asking. What are some of the activities for children in [college town]?"

Tenure Is Not a Reward

So far, we've been discussing getting a job. Let's say you succeed and get on the tenure track. Go back and reread the last chapter for advice about working effectively and productively, with good time-management skills. Then come back to this section, specifically about getting tenure.

Remember how tenure works. You start as an assistant professor on "probation" for six or seven years. At the end of that period, you are required to apply for promotion to associate professor with tenure. What it takes to get tenure varies from school to school. At some places, promotion depends entirely or almost entirely on research output; at others, it depends mostly on teaching and service.

How elaborate the process is also varies. Some universities will solicit ten outside evaluation letters assessing the quality of your research. Your application will pass through seven or eight votes (a subcommittee in your department, your entire department, your school's promotion committee, your entire school's senior faculty, the university rank and promotion committee, the provost, the president, the board of trustees). At others, tenure approval might take only two or three steps. At some schools, the process takes over ten months; at others, only two or three months.

If you succeed, you're awarded tenure and promoted to associate professor. Congratulations! You now have one of the most secure jobs in the world for as long as you want. If you fail, you are usually granted a "terminal" year—a one-year extension on your contract. You can keep teaching and working for one more year (perhaps with a demotion and salary cut) to help get your affairs together and apply for other jobs. After that, your job at that university ends. You're fired. Up or out. This is the "perish" part of "publish or perish."

Tenure is not a *reward*.[6] It is not a reward for time served or services rendered. It is not an assessment of your character or likeability. It's not given to you in exchange for what you've done for the school. Instead, tenure is a *hire*.

Remember, if the university wants an associate professor, it doesn't need to hire an assistant professor, give him six years, and then promote him. It could instead hire an already tenured associate professor directly from another university. So, when your college or university decides to tenure you, what they are really deciding is this: Suppose we wanted to hire an associate professor in this field with whatever salary budget we have. Could we reasonably expect to get someone *better* than you, the assistant professor currently applying for tenure? If the answer is yes, then you probably won't get tenure. (They can just advertise and hire someone better.) If the answer is no, then you probably will.

Your job as an assistant professor is to make sure the answer is no. When you apply for tenure, you are competing for an associate professorship job against all the other possible people the university could instead recruit. This means that if the university generally wants six A-level publications for tenure, you get ten instead. You teach better than your colleagues do. You do more service than you're expected to do. Aim for standards much higher than the university expects, and you'll be a sure thing.

Tenure is not a reward for what you've done, but a job offered on the basis of whom they expect you to be for the rest of your career.

Is There a Job Shortage?

For as long as I've been in academia, everyone's complained about a job shortage. For one nitpicky reason and one substantive reason, that's not quite right.

The nitpicky reason: If you're an economist, you probably know what I'm about to say. When the quantity supplied of something exceeds the quantity demanded, there is a glut, not a shortage. The number of people offering themselves up for academic jobs (quantity supplied) exceeds the number of job openings (quantity demanded). *Shortage* is the wrong word.

Now for the more substantive reason. You might think, okay, sure, technically, it's a glut, not a shortage. But, you might think, isn't the reason that quantity supplied exceeds quantity demanded is that universities are cutting jobs, hiring fewer and fewer people? Aren't the ranks of tenure-track and full-time jobs shrinking? Isn't it really a demand-side problem, not a supply-side problem? That's what I hear from adjuncts' rights activists, op-ed writers in the *Chronicle*, and many senior faculty.

Answer to all three questions: Nope.

The US Department of Education collects and publishes excellent statistics about how many people hold academic jobs of various sorts and ranks in the United States. Figure 4.1 shows you the total number of people employed in the US as *assistant professors* since 2002. This number does not include lecturers, adjuncts, part-time professors, instructors, or other junior job holders. As you can see, the number of assistant

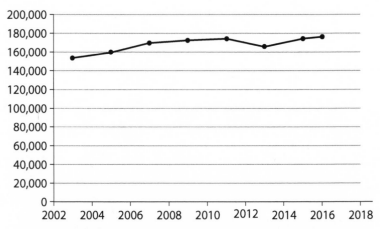

Figure 4.1. Number of people employed as assistant professors per year since 2002. US Department of Education, IPEDS, tables 239 and 315.20.

professors has generally grown, even during and after the Great Recession.

For what it's worth, the number of people employed as assistant professors grew faster than the number of people employed as senior faculty. So, one story I hear—"The jobs dried up because the senior faculty refused to retire after the Great Recession"—doesn't hold up either.

Figure 4.2 shows the ratio of all full-time faculty to students in the United States since 1970. As you can see, the ratio of full-time faculty to students has remained more or less constant since 1970 and is actually better now than it was in the 1980s.

In *Cracks in the Ivory Tower*, Phil Magness and I examined these trends. Conventional wisdom holds that humanities jobs are being cut, which in turn explains why the market for English or modern language professors is so bad. It's the same number of students chasing ever fewer jobs. If the jobs kept pace with student enrollments, then most PhDs would get decent faculty jobs.

On the contrary, we discovered a different set of trends.

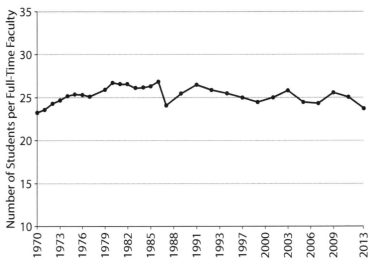

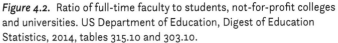

Figure 4.2. Ratio of full-time faculty to students, not-for-profit colleges and universities. US Department of Education, Digest of Education Statistics, 2014, tables 315.10 and 303.10.

First, the rate of growth of jobs in the humanities is *faster* than the rate of growth in many other more financially stable fields, such as economics. For instance, take a look at figures 4.3 and 4.4, derived from the Bureau of Labor Statistics and US Department of Education data. Figure 4.3 shows you the number of full-time English faculty compared to the number of bachelor's degrees in English issued each year. Figure 4.4 does the same for economics.[7]

Student demand for English degrees is down, but nevertheless, English's presence on campus has been getting larger. English is growing faster than economics, even though demand for economics degrees is up. The other humanities show similar trends. In fact, overall, faculty positions in the humanities have grown more and at a faster rate than positions in any other field except for those in the health sciences, such as nursing.[8] There are at least 40% more humanities professors now than in 1999.

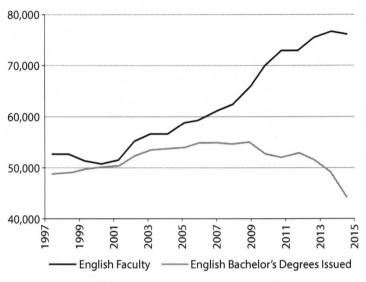

Figure 4.3. English faculty growth over time. Brennan and Magness 2019, 166.

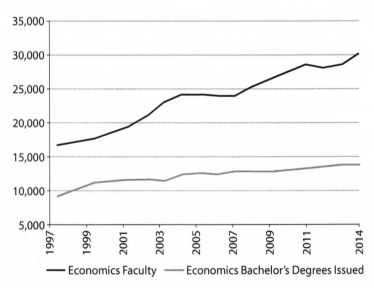

Figure 4.4. Economics faculty growth over time. Brennan and Magness 2019, 166.

Keep in mind that in many colleges and universities, money follows students. The more students taking classes in your department, the more money your department receives. You get $X per butt in seat and $Y per student major. Not all colleges follow this system (mine doesn't), but for those that do, many of their humanities departments are put in a precarious position. Humanities departments in the United States tend to have a high faculty-to-student ratio. For example, across the country, the overall faculty-per-undergrad degree ratio is 1.93 in foreign languages and 1.71 in English. It's only 0.23 in business, 0.30 in engineering, and 0.42 in economics.

Maybe English has the right number of faculty and economics has too few; I don't know how to determine that. However, for the sake of argument, imagine that deans around the country decide to cut their English departments in order to get the 0.5 faculty-to-degree ratio the social sciences exhibit. This would require only 22,000 English faculty to service 44,000 bachelor's degrees per year. They'd have to lay off 53,000 English professors to reach parity with other core departments.[9]

This partly explains why English professors get paid less than economics professors: they have a higher faculty-to-student ratio overall. If you gave them both an equal salary pool to split among their hires, English profs would get less than economists. (That's not the whole story, of course. Part of the reason economics profs get paid more is that universities have to compete with banks, government, finance, and other sectors that are willing to hire econ PhDs.)

The second trend we noticed is that the number of PhDs granted in most fields has been increasing. There was a giant boom in the golden years of the late 1960s, followed by a mass drop in the 1980s. But since the 1990s, most fields have produced ever more PhDs, as figure 4.5 illustrates.

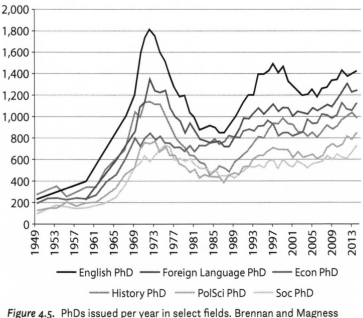

Figure 4.5. PhDs issued per year in select fields. Brennan and Magness 2019, 191.

Putting all this (plus some other data) together, what we found surprised us: the overall problem with the academic job market isn't that jobs are drying up, lines are being cut, full-timers are being replaced by part-timers, or that jobs fail to keep pace with student enrollments. Instead, the overall national trend is that lines are being added, the full-timers keep up with the students, and the number of jobs per undergraduate student is increasing *faster* in the humanities than in most other fields, despite declining demand for humanities degrees. The real reason there is a surplus of humanities PhDs is that humanities departments graduate ever more PhDs each year, generally at a faster rate than the rate of job growth. An overproduction of PhDs leads to an oversupply of job seekers. The problem is not a drop in demand or quantity demanded for humanities jobs.[10] It's a supply-side problem.

What does this mean for you? First, if you can choose between multiple academic fields, all things being equal, you should pick the financially stable fields with low PhD-to-job ratios and low faculty-to-degree ratios. If you're indifferent between English and sociology, pick sociology. If you're indifferent between economics and sociology, pick economics. If you're indifferent between political theory and American government, pick American government.

Is the Market Going to Get Worse Due to the Threat of Online Education?

Doom and gloom! Academia is over! No one is safe! Don't bother to get a PhD, because the jobs are going to disappear! Universities as we know them will largely cease to exist in the next twenty years! Online education will take over and replace the traditional four-year college!

I've been hearing such predictions for twenty-plus years, and I expect I'll keep hearing them for another twenty. You've probably heard them, too. Should you be worried? I'm not, and I don't think you should be. I expect financial problems will cause some smaller liberal arts colleges on the margins to close. But I doubt online education will supplant traditional four-year colleges anytime soon.

The question here is what drives student demand for the four-year degree. Sorry to sound crass, but for the most part, it's not love of liberal learning for liberal learning's sake. After all, few people buy philosophy books, books on critical theory, translations of the classics, or whatnot, on their own, outside of being assigned such books for class. Demand for such products is low, which is evidence that most people aren't interested in liberal learning for its own sake.

If people really loved education for education's sake, you'd have dozens of inquiries per semester from neighbors asking if they might secretly sit in on your classes for free—and you'd have people trying to do so without asking. How often does that happen to you? I've had it happen once, and I'm something of a public intellectual.

Instead, for the most part, people go to college because a college degree brings a significant wage premium. In the United States, college graduates earn on average $17,500 more per year than people with only a high school diploma.[11] A college degree is a necessary condition for getting many desirable jobs, the kinds of jobs that make you middle or upper-middle class. People with four-year degrees have lower unemployment rates than those with less education.[12]

The interesting question here is *why* college graduates receive a college wage premium. Knowing the answer will help us determine whether and how much online education is a threat.

In economics, there are two basic theories, or hypotheses, about what causes the college wage premium:

1 *The Human Capital Theory.* This is the theory colleges put in their brochures and advertisements. According to this theory, college imparts a wide range of marketable skills, such as good writing, critical thinking, creative thinking, organization, ability to synthesize ideas, and so on. College makes students more productive, and so graduates earn a higher wage. College turns you into the right stuff.

2 *The Signaling Theory.* A college degree is a sorting mechanism. Employers need to separate the wheat from the chaff. To acquire a college degree requires students to endure and survive a sometimes extremely difficult admissions process and then endure and pass

four years' worth of often challenging classes. That a person completes college proves to potential employers that she has a combination of desirable traits: she is smart, perseverant, conscientious, and conforms to society's expectations (isn't too weird). College proves you have the right stuff.

These theories are compatible in the sense that the wage premium may be explained by both. Maybe it's 50% human capital development and 50% signaling, or some other mix. The most thorough investigation of these two theories is economist Bryan Caplan's recent book, *The Case against Education*.[13] That title might miff you, but if you're worried about jobs, you'll like his argument. Caplan scrupulously examines the various predictions each theory makes about how people consume education and how finishing college versus dropping out after three years affects wages, about social versus private returns, about how much students learn in college and whether the research shows that they can apply college skills outside the classroom, and so on.

The evidence is fairly depressing: Students don't learn much. They don't transfer their skills. Dropping out a week before you finish college gets you little more wage premium than if you never went at all—you get a serious wage premium only if you finish. All this is predicted by the Signaling Theory, not the Human Capital Theory. So, Caplan concludes, something like 80% of the wage premium comes from signaling.

That is depressing, because it's evidence that liberal education doesn't work the way we professors want to believe it works. But it's also wonderful news for academic job security. If the wage premium comes from signaling, then online education isn't a good competitor for traditional education. Online education does a far worse job signaling that a student is smart, perseverant, and conformist. It doesn't prove as much that a person will meet society's expectations, will jump through hoops, and will perform pointless exercises on command. Indeed, the efficiency of online education actually reduces the quality of its signal. For the signal to work, education has to be tedious, difficult, and long.

Here's another way to think of it: If online education were a serious threat, it should already have done more damage. Most Americans have good internet connections and a variety of smart devices. Online education nevertheless remains at the margins.

Is There a Bias against Conservatives?

In general, in most fields, people seen as being on the Right will have a harder time than others getting hired, promoted, or published.

You probably know the statistics that academia is skewed leftward compared to the general public. In the early 1990s, 20% of faculty identified as conservative, 40% as moderate, and 40% as left-wing. Now the numbers are about 10% conservative, 30% moderate, and 60% left-wing.[14] In certain fields, people on the Left outnumber people on the Right by a factor of 25:1 or higher.

These numbers may reflect changing labels as well as people's changing views. For instance, *conservative* today might connote some affiliation with Donald Trump. For that reason, people who would have called themselves conservative ten years ago might use a different label today.

Scholars debate just why academia is skewed leftward. Some claim that a conservative mindset is incompatible with academic work. They argue that conservativism by definition or in practice discourages the critical thinking, detachment, suspicion, and the willingness to overturn convention that academic work requires.[15] (To conservatives, I suspect that this sounds like a fancier version of the "conservatives are too dumb to work in academia" argument.)

Perhaps it's a partly self-reinforcing selection effect. Plenty of research shows that people in general prefer to live near, befriend, and work with people who share their politics.[16] Most people self-segregate by ideology when they can. Conservatives know the academy skews leftward, so they pursue academic work at lower rates. Leftists want to work with leftists, and are thus likelier to pursue academic work. Over time, such selection effects cause the academy to skew ever leftward. On this model, had academia leaned slightly rightward as of 1960, we'd expect it to be extremely right-leaning today. Given what we know about ideological self-segregation, this model must explain at least some of the disparity.

However, there is empirical evidence of straight-up, explicit discrimination in hiring. First, there is ample evidence that in general, people discriminate against and mistreat people who have different political views from their own, and that the more strongly one is interested in politics, the nastier one tends to be to those with different political opinions.[17] There's no reason to think academics are immune to the general trend.

To illustrate, consider a famous experiment by political scientists Shanto Iyengar and Sean Westwood. They asked more than a thousand subjects to evaluate what they were told were the résumés of graduating high school students. The résumés were written so that some were objectively stronger than others, and were also tagged with various political affiliations. This experiment allowed Iyengar and Westwood to measure how much people are inclined to discriminate in favor of their own political tribes. The results: 80.4% of Democratic subjects picked the Democratic job candidate, while 69.2% of

Republican subjects picked the Republican job candidate. Even when the Republican job candidate was clearly stronger, Democrats still chose the Democratic candidate 70% of the time. (Republicans weren't much better.) In contrast, the research finds that "candidate qualification had no significant effect on winner section."[18]

In another famous survey, Yoel Inbar and Joris Lammers asked academic psychologists whether they would discriminate against conservatives in hiring. They found that a large number admitted they would discriminate in hiring and peer review decisions; the more left-wing they were, they more they admitted they would discriminate. Still, even in their survey, most respondents described themselves as not likely to discriminate, while a sizable minority admitted they would discriminate (and rather significantly). However, for hiring decisions, over 44% admitted they would be strongly likely to discriminate. At least a third admitted the same for refereeing papers and grants.[19]

There is a phenomenon called "social desirability bias." People answer anonymous surveys in ways that make them look good. They exaggerate their good attributes and understate their bad attributes. In an anonymous survey, if 44% of psychologists admit they'd discriminate against conservative job candidates, the real number will be higher than 44%. If psychologists give themselves a mean discriminatory rating of 3.5 on a 7-point scale, then the real number will be higher. These are lower bounds.[20]

In a paper in the *Harvard Journal of Law and Public Policy*, James Cleith Phillips provides strong evidence that libertarian and conservative law professors must publish more and achieve more than their peers in order to obtain equivalent academic positions. Libertarian and conservative law professors tend to be cited more often, and publish more often and in more prestigious venues, than their peers with identical ranks at the same law schools.[21]

Imagine learning that black professors are a small minority at the top sixteen law schools. Further, you discover the black professors tend to have more publications in better, higher-ranked outlets, get cited more, give more presentations, and in general have more impressive CVs than their equally ranked white peers at the same institutions. It's plausible to conclude that black professors had to *achieve more* to obtain the same jobs as their less accomplished white peers, which is evidence that they had to overcome discrimination and that the white professors had it easier.[22] I'm not saying that people on the Left are especially bad, by the way. If, in some alternative universe, academia had come to be dominated by Republicans, I'd expect they would behave the same way.

On the Difficulty of Disagreeing with the Consensus

There's a broader point here, which applies not merely to conservatives. Any person with a point of view different from what's normal in his field will face an uphill battle.

One reason is that ideology tells you which problems are important and which are not. For instance, in sociology, it's easier to get a paper on inequality published than a paper on the empirical effects of economic freedom, because people's background ideologies tell them to care about the first question more than the second. It's easier to publish a paper blaming differences in life outcomes on social factors than on IQ. In other fields, it goes the other way.

If you go against the mainstream view in your field, journal referees are likelier to reject your basic premises and will work harder to find holes in and problems with your argument. They are less likely to do so if they agree with you. This holds not just for left-versus-right divides, but any time you challenge the consensus view.

The bad news for you is that challenging the consensus view on any topic takes extra hard work. The good news is that you'll by necessity have to produce better work than you otherwise would. Discrimination and disagreement may well kill you, but if you survive, at least your work will be stronger as a result.

UPSHOTS

- Most job markets are centralized, and the entire process, from advertising to hiring, takes about nine to ten months complete.
- Although an application may be one hundred pages long, most applications will get only a short scan. The opening page of every part of the application must have a hook. Whatever is most interesting or impressive about you goes on page 1.
- Most dossiers are boring. Yours shouldn't be.
- Your CV tells a story about you. There are certain mistakes to avoid and certain stories you want it to tell.
- Have a pitch for your dissertation, but also for what you plan to do five and ten years from now.
- Be prepared to interview for an hour about any line on your CV.
- Certain interview questions are more important than they sound at first glance. Don't punt on them. Be prepared to deal with weird, illegal, and inappropriate questions.
- Committees hire professionals, not students. Getting a job means proving you can do the job.
- Committees want to hire people they'll like having around. Be collegial.
- Tenure is a hire, not a reward.
- In most fields, there is no job shortage. There is instead a glut of PhDs. Yes, this distinction makes a difference. The number of jobs has kept pace with student enrollments, but PhD programs have increased the number of degrees they award.
- Online education poses little threat to traditional four-year schools, at least for now, because it doesn't provide the same kind of signal.
- People with unconventional views, as well as people with unpopular political views, will on average have a harder time

publishing and getting jobs than others. There is both explicit and implicit discrimination.

- The unemployment rate for PhDs is low, even though most of them don't get faculty jobs. You can start preparing for other jobs your first year of grad school.
- To call the job market a lottery is not only false counsel but also poisonous advice. People who say that have an agenda, and it's not helping you succeed.

Exit Options

THE AVERAGE PERSON who gets a PhD will not get a long-term faculty job. Faculty jobs are the nail for which the PhD is the hammer. Yet—to extend that metaphor—half the people who reach for the hammer never pick it up. Half who swing it miss the nail. But don't sweat it. It turns out you can repurpose this hammer to do all sorts of other work.

According to the Bureau of Labor Statistics, the unemployment rate in the United States for master's degree holders in 2015 was 2.4%, and for PhD holders, 1.7%.[1] These are astoundingly low numbers.

The people who quit academia usually do well in the long run. Some academic researchers have studied what happens to PhDs after they give up looking for faculty jobs. They find jobs all over the place, as academic administrators, as editors or journalists, as high school teachers, in NGOs, working in government, or in any number of professional jobs in private business.[2] Most people who get a PhD do not end up securing a long-term academic position, and yet the majority do find good, decent-paying, full-time professional employment elsewhere.[3]

Many of these jobs are as rewarding as working in academia. Getting a job outside academia isn't failure.

How to use your PhD to get a job outside academia depends on the kind of job you're pursuing. I won't try to offer advice here. There's so much variation in what employers want that there's no useful summary.

Instead, let me offer advice about *when* to start looking elsewhere. If you are at a graduate program that rarely places students in long-term faculty jobs, then you are unlikely to get a long-term faculty job. Thus, you should be researching, thinking about, and preparing your CV—including acquiring the right kinds of credentials and accomplishments—for these jobs right away, starting your first year of grad school. When you go on the academic job market, you should simultaneously apply for other kinds of jobs. Don't wait until the professorship job market cycle ends and then hope to grab something. You might be stuck for months with nothing.

One thing you can and should do—regardless of how prestigious your program is—is go to your university's career center.[4] The counselors there probably have ample resources for you and can help mentor you—and network you—in finding nonprofessoriate employment with your PhD. Go ahead and meet with them in your first year of graduate school. They can help you determine what sorts of jobs you might like and how you can best prepare for these jobs. They'll probably also be delighted to help you, because PhD students so rarely take advantage of the help they offer.

If you don't get a long-term academic job on the first go-around, you might be able to stick it out as a postdoc, a visiting assistant professor, or an adjunct, and then try again. Being a postdoc in itself can help increase your chances; being a VAP or an adjunct probably won't. Regardless, you've got to spend your time improving your CV and credentials, say, by publishing more and better. Every year you go through the process, your PhD gets "staler," so your other credentials have to be better.

How many shots should you take? How many years should you hang on and keep applying for faculty jobs before giving up? That's up to you. It depends on how badly you want it and how many years of income and security you're willing to give up. My best recommendation, though, is to set a clear "number" ahead of time—"I'll go through three cycles then move on"—rather than leave it as a year-to-year decision. Start planning for your exit early, and stick to your number. Whatever your preferred exit option is, find the equivalent of this book for that option, read it, and start planning. There's lots of good work out there, if you can get it.

ACKNOWLEDGMENTS

Thanks to Zak Slayback, who interviewed me in 2017 about how to be productive in academia for his *Doers* podcast. That interview and a corresponding short article I wrote for his website formed the basis of this book. Thanks to Matt McAdam, my editor at Johns Hopkins University Press, for suggesting that I write this book and for his helpful guidance along the way. Thanks to two anonymous referees for their feedback and suggestions. Thanks to David Schmidtz, Michael Munger, Tyler Cowen, and John Tomasi. I benefited as a grad student from attending their professionalization workshops. Many of the best ideas in this book come from them and from their mentors (such as Douglass North or Allen Buchanan), in turn. Finally, thanks to my mom, who taught me that even if many things are outside your control, you'll do your best if you maintain an internal locus of control.

NOTES

Introduction. Unpleasant Truths about the World's Best Job

1. Rogers 2013, 9.
2. Cassuto 2013; https://www.nsf.gov/statistics/2018/nsf18304
/datatables/tab44.htm; https://www.nsf.gov/statistics/2018/nsf18304
/datatables/tab46.htm. The Survey of Earned Doctorates indicates that
in 2016, only about 61% of recent PhDs had firm commitments of *any* sort
upon graduation. Of those with commitments, only 44.6% had commitments in academia, though this number includes tenure-track professorships, non-tenure-track professorships, postdoctoral fellowships, and
academic administration/support. So, off the bat, only about 13% of
people who enter a PhD program can expect to get *some* sort of job at a
university, let alone a tenure-track professorship.
3. See Cassuto 2013. The best available data are found in the NSF's
Survey of Earned Doctorates. That survey indicates that only about 26%
of PhD graduates have any sort of academic job upon graduation. Since
roughly half of first-year PhD students do not finish, we can cut that
number in half. But it's hard to know how many of the people with no
professorship job upon graduation finally end up with a professorship. On
the other hand, the survey includes administrative and non-tenure-track
jobs as academic jobs. See also Larson, Ghaffarzadegan, and Xue 2014,
which gives us an estimate closer to 20%, including non-tenure-track jobs.
4. See Lodge and Taber 2013.
5. See Brennan and Magness 2019, chap. 8.
6. See Brennan and Magness, 2019; Brennan and Magness 2018a;
Brennan and Magness 2018b.

Chapter 1. Do You Really Want an Academic Job?

1. Flaherty 2018a. It's unclear how much of this is a selection-versus-
treatment effect.
2. National Center for Educational Statistics, https://nces.ed.gov
/fastfacts /display.asp?id=84.
3. https://philosophy.georgetown.edu/graduate/phd-graduates
/placement-record.
4. Ziker 2014.

5. https://academics.boisestate.edu/provost/files/2013/02/Anthropology-Work-Load-Policy-1.pdf.

6. Ziker 2014.

7. http://carnegieclassifications.iu.edu/lookup/view_institution.php?unit_id=142115.

8. US Department of Education, IPEDS, table 315.30. Note: these findings were also consistent with an earlier, 1994 AAUP study, itself based on earlier Department of Education data going back to 1987. See Rosenthal 1994. Similar attestations of faculty time allocation may be found in the 2010–11 Higher Education Research Institute survey (Hurtado et al. 2011), esp. 26–27. The consistency of these studies suggests that full-time faculty teaching obligations have remained relatively stable for several decades.

9. US Department of Education, IPEDS, table 315.30. See also Hurtado et al. 2011, 26–27, which suggests a similar increase in teaching-related time allocation for faculty at four-year colleges when compared to full universities.

10. Jenkins 2016.

11. Gross and Simmons 2007.

12. Most schools offer failed tenure applicants a one-year contract to keep them afloat while they find work elsewhere.

13. For more on the problem of bloated administrations, see Ginsberg 2013.

14. For a comprehensive review of the problems with student teaching evaluations, see Brennan and Magness 2019, chap. 4.

15. Brogaard, Engelberg, and van Wesep, 2017; Goodwin and Sauer 1995; Holley 1977; Lewis 1980; Williams and Ceci 2007.

16. Coalition on the Academic Workforce 22 Survey, http://www.academicworkforce.org /CAW_portrait_2012.pdf.

17. The 2012 Coalition on the Academic Workforce survey found that only 30% of adjunct respondents possessed a completed doctorate. A more extensive analysis conducted in 2003 by the US Department of Education showed that about 18% of adjuncts held doctorates. The largest category in both studies was a master's degree. See CAW table 9 and IPEDS table 315.70; The Higher Education Research Institute at UCLA found in a 2010 survey of undergraduate faculty that only 24% of adjuncts held a PhD, while an additional 4% held terminal equivalents, such as an EdD, an MD, or a DDS. See Hurtado et al. 2011, 173. The American Federation of Teachers 2010 survey similarly found that only 26% of adjuncts held a PhD.

18. Brennan and Magness 2018a; US Department of Education, Digest of Education Statistics, tables 315.10 and 303.10.

19. Magness 2016.

20. https://nces.ed.gov/programs/coe/indicator_csc.asp.

21. https://www.agb.org/trusteeship/2013/5/changing-academic
-workforce. .

22. https://www.aaup.org/sites/default/files/ARES_2017-18.pdf.

23. https://www.aaup.org/sites/default/files/ARES_2017-18.pdf,
table 6.

24. https://nces.ed.gov/programs/coe/indicator_csc.asp.

25. https://www.insidehighered.com/aaup-compensation-survey.

26. https://www.insidehighered.com/aaup-compensation-survey
?institution-name=&professor-category=1601&order=field_avg
_salary&sort=desc.

27. https://www.aaup.org/sites/default/files/ARES_2017-18.pdf,
table 7.

28. Calculations made using https://www.nerdwallet.com/cost-of
-living-calculator/compare/st-louis-mo-il-vs-boston-ma.

29. http://www.businessinsider.com/us-census-median-income-2017-9;
https://www.census.gov/data/tables/time-series/demo/income-poverty
/historical-income-households.html.

30. Jaschik 2015.

31. Dixon 2017.

32. The Quad, "The Ten Highest-Paid College Professors in the US,"
http://www.thebestschools.org/blog/2013/11/25/10-highest-paid-college
-professors-u-s/.

33. Read 2015.

34. Brennan and Magness 2019, 38.

35. Larson, Ghaffarzadegan, and Xue 2014.

36. Jeremy Fox, "Don't Worry Too Much about Whether You'll Get
Tenure, because You Probably Will," https://dynamicecology.wordpress
.com/2014/07/21/dont-worry-too-much-about-whether-youll-get-tenure
-because-you-probably-will/.

37. https://www.chronicle.com/article/Full-Time-Instructional
/148195.

38. https://www.chronicle.com/article/PhD-Attrition-How-Much-Is
/140045.

39. Surprenant also warns against the "GoPro Fallacy," which is the
fallacy of thinking that if you spend enough on a fancy camera, someone
will want to watch your videos.

40. To be more precise, if all you know about someone is that she's a
PhD student, you might conclude that she has a 50% chance of finishing, a
20% chance of getting any long-term faculty job, and a 12%–13% chance
of getting a tenure-track job. But most people have additional information
about themselves, such as the quality and placement record of their
department, the job prospects in their field, and so on, which make these
overall percentages a bad estimate for them. A PhD student in the top
academic department might have a 70% chance of getting a tenure-track

job at graduation, whereas a student in the 100th ranked department has a 0% chance.

41. https://www.heri.ucla.edu/monographs/HERI-FAC2014 -monograph-expanded.pdf, 30.

42. https://www.heri.ucla.edu/monographs/HERI-FAC2014 -monograph-expanded.pdf, 30, authors' calculations.

43. https://www.heri.ucla.edu/monographs/HERI-FAC2014 -monograph-expanded.pdf, 29, authors' calculations.

44. https://www.heri.ucla.edu/monographs/HERI-FAC2014 -monograph-expanded.pdf, 29. authors' calculations. To get this low estimate, I assume that all the surveyed faculty in the lower categories hit the maximum for their category, and all the surveyed faculty in the two higher categories hit the minimum. This gives us a ratio of the top two groups having published 684.3 papers for every 412.8 the bottom five groups published.

45. https://journals.aps.org/prl/issues/121/26.

46. https://www.chronicle.com/article/Can-It-Really-Be-True-That /243564.

47. This blogpost has the relevant statistics and links to evidence for these claims: http://blogs.lse.ac.uk/impactofsocialsciences/2014/04/23 /academic-papers-citation-rates-remler/.

48. https://nces.ed.gov/fastfacts/display.asp?id=171.

49. https://blog.prepscholar.com/what-is-the-average-sat-score.

50. Arum and Roksa 2011.

51. Arum and Roksa 2011, 35-36.

52. Arum and Roksa 2011, 121.

53. Arum and Roksa 2011, 219n15.

54. https://www.myplan.com/careers/top-ten/highest-job -satisfaction.php; Adams 2013.

Chapter 2. Success in Graduate School Means Working to Get a Job

1. https://www.prepscholar.com/gre/blog/average-gre-scores/.

2. Hersch 2014.

3. For instance, read the sordid tale of Avital Ronell at the Departments of German and of Comparative Literature at NYU: Chu 2018; Greenberg 2018. In addition to sexually harassing at least one student, Ronell seems to have managed to eliminate the requirement that PhD students in German demonstrate—get this—proficiency in German, and instead mandated that all student work cite *her*.

4. Colander and Zhuo 2015.

5. O'Shaughnessy 2012.

6. *Chronicle of Higher Education*, Almanac, 2015-16, 4, https://www .chronicle.com /specialreport/The-Almanac-of-Higher/4.

7. It's surprisingly difficult to come up with a book-length research topic. It's relatively easy to think of a thirty-page project, akin to "Here's an application of one argument Derrida made in one paper." It's easy to think of a three-thousand-page project, akin to "I want to write a comprehensive history of the Songhai Empire." Finding a manageable, original idea in between turns out to be hard. Most ideas are either too little or too big.

8. O'Shaughnessy 2012.

9. Flaherty 2018b.

10. Herrmann 2016.

Chapter 3. How to Be Productive and Happy

1. McMahan 2017.

2. MacFarquhar 2011.

3. In chapter 1, I mentioned that faculty at many R2 and R3 universities were working sixty hours a week. In their case, I'm not sure how much this has to do with imperfect time management and how much with their having a sort of "worst of both worlds" problem: they have to try to publish like R1 professors but teach as much as liberal arts professors.

4. Hollis et al. 2008.

5. I get these from David Schmidtz, and much of this section comes from him.

6. I get this from Mike Munger, who got it from James Buchanan.

7. Munger 2005, 21.

8. Thanks to David Schmidtz for some version of this analogy.

9. Munger 2005, 25

10. Brennan 2012.

11. Brennan and Jaworski 2015; Brennan and Jaworski 2016.

12. Ginsberg 2013.

13. "Estimated Class Sizes: More than 90 National Universities," http://publicuniversityhonors.com/2015/10/20/estimated-class-sizes-more-than-90-national-universities/.

Chapter 4. The Academic Market, Tenure, and the Job Market outside Academia

1. *Chronicle of Higher Education*, "Almanac, 2015-16," 41.

2. Gale, Batty, and Deary 2008.

3. Dana, Dawes, and Peterson 2013; Kausel, Culbertson, and Madrid 2016; Arvey and Campion 1982; Pulakos and Schmitt 1995.

4. https://twitter.com/ethanbdm/status/1086648540879835136.

5. Thanks to David Schmidtz for this line.

6. This point and the ideas in the next few paragraphs all come from Mike Munger.

7. Occupational Employment Survey, Bureau of Labor Statistics, 2015; Digest of Education Statistics, sec. 325.

8. https://www.humanitiesindicators.org/content/indicatordoc.aspx?i=319.

9. Reprinted from Brennan and Magness 2019, 168.

10. Brennan and Magness 2019, chap. 8.

11. Dewan 2014.

12. Bureau of Labor Statistics, https://www.bls.gov/opub/ted/2018/unemployment-rate-2-1-percent-for-college-grads-3-9-percent-for-high-school-grads-in-august-2018.htm?view_full.

13. Caplan 2018.

14. Abrams 2016.

15. Cholbi 2014.

16. Mutz 2006.

17. Brennan 2016.

18. Iyengar and Westwood 2015.

19. Inbar and Lammers 2012.

20. Inbar and Lammers 2012

21. Phillips 2016.

22. If you'd like to know about what it's like to be a conservative in academia, I suggest reading Jon Shields and Joshua Dunn's *Passing on the Right*. It provides a sober and fair-minded analysis. For the most part, universities are not cartoonish bastions of leftist intolerance and indoctrination. Nevertheless, many conservative academics are treated badly for their politics.

Conclusion. **Exit Options**

1. Bureau of Labor Statistics, http://www.bls.gov/emp/ep_chart_001.htm. This appears to count full-time employment.

2. Rogers 2013.

3. Nerad, Aanerud, and Cerny 1999.

4. Thanks to Matt McAdam for this point.

BIBLIOGRAPHY

Databases and Surveys
American Academy of Arts and Sciences. Humanities Indicators. https://www.humanitiesindicators.org/default.aspx.
American Association of University Professors. Annual Report of the Economic Status of the Profession. https://www.aaup.org/sites /default/files/ARES_2017-18.pdf.
American Federation of Teachers. American Academic Survey of Part-Time Faculty, 2010. https://www.aft.org/sites/default/files/aa _partimefaculty0310.pdf.
Chronicle of Higher Education. Almanacs. https://www.chronicle.com /specialreport/The-Almanac-of-Higher/4.
Chronicle of Higher Education. Chronicle Data. https://data.chronicle.com /category/sector/2/faculty-salaries/.
Coalition on the Academic Workforce. http://www.academicworkforce.org.
Higher Education Research Institute. HERI Faculty Surveys. https://heri .ucla.edu/heri-faculty-survey.
Inside Higher Ed. AAUP Compensation Surveys. https://www .insidehighered.com/aaup-compensation-survey.
National Science Foundation. National Center for Science and Engineering Statistics. Survey of Earned Doctorates. https://www.nsf.gov/statistics/.
US Census Bureau. https://www.census.gov/data.
US Department of Education. Institute of Education Sciences, National Center for Educational Statistics. Digest of Education Statistics. https://nces.ed.gov/.
US Department of Education. Institute of Education Sciences, National Center for Educational Statistics. Integrated Postsecondary Education Data System. https://nces.ed.gov/ipeds/.
US Department of Labor. Bureau of Labor Statistics. Occupational Employment Survey. https://www.bls.gov/.

Published Works
Abrams, Sam. 2016. "Professors Moved Left since the 1990s, Rest of America Did Not." https://heterodoxacademy.org/professors-moved -left-but-country-did-not/.

Adams, Susan. 2013. "The Least Stressful Jobs of 2013." *Forbes*, Jan. 3. https://www.forbes.com/sites/susanadams/2013/01/03/the-least -stressful-jobs-of-2013/#23f7827f6e24.

Arum, Richard, and Josipa Roksa. 2011. *Academically Adrift: Limited Learning on College Campuses*. Chicago: University of Chicago Press.

Arvey, Richard D., and James E. Campion. 1982. "The Employment Interview: A Summary and Review of Recent Research." *Personnel Psychology* 35: 281–322.

Brennan, Jason. 2012. "Political Liberty: Who Needs It?" *Social Philosophy and Policy* 29: 1–27.

———. 2016. *Against Democracy*. Princeton: Princeton University Press.

Brennan, Jason, and Peter Jaworski. 2015. "Markets without Symbolic Limits." *Ethics* 125: 1053–1077.

———. 2016. *Markets without Limits*. New York: Routledge Press.

Brennan, Jason, and Phillip Magness. 2018a. "Estimating the Cost of Justice for Adjuncts: A Case Study in University Business Ethics." *Journal of Business Ethics* 148: 155–168.

———. 2018b. "Are Adjunct Faculty Exploited? Some Grounds for Skepticism." *Journal of Business Ethics* 152: 53–71.

———. 2019. *Cracks in the Ivory Tower: The Moral Mess of Higher Education*. New York: Oxford University Press.

Brogaard, Jonathan, Joseph Engelberg, and Edward van Wesep. 2017. "Do Economists Swing for the Fences after Tenure?" Available at SSRN: https://papers.ssrn.com/sol3.

Caplan, Bryan. 2018. *The Case against Education*. Princeton: Princeton University Press.

Cassuto, Leonard. 2013. "PhD Attrition: How Much Is Too Much?" *Chronicle of Higher Education*, July 1. https://www.chronicle.com/ article/PhD-Attrition-How-Much-Is/140045.

Cholbi, Michael. 2014. "Anti-Conservative Bias in Education Is Real—But Not Unjust." *Social Philosophy and Policy* 31: 176–203.

Chu, Andrea Long. 2018. "I Worked with Avital Ronell. I Believe Her Accuser." *Chronicle of Higher Education*, Aug. 30. https://www .chronicle.com/article/I-Worked-With-Avital-Ronell-I/244415.

Colander, David, and Daisy Zhuo. 2015. "Where Do PhDs in English Get Jobs? An Economist's View of the English PhD Market." *Pedagogy: Critical Approaches to Teaching Literature, Language, Composition, and Culture* 15: 139–156.

Council of Graduate Schools. 2012. "US Graduate Schools Report Slight Growth in New Students for Fall 2012." https://cgsnet.org/us-graduate -schools-report-slight-growth-new-students-fall-2012.

Dana, Jason, Robyn Dawes, and Nathanial Peterson. 2013. "Belief in the Unstructured Interview: The Persistence of an Illusion." *Judgment and Decision Making* 8: 512.

Dewan, Shaila. 2014. "Wage Premium from College Is Said to Be Up." *New York Times*, Feb. 11. https://economix.blogs.nytimes.com/2014/02/11/wage-premium-from-college-is-said-to-be-up/.

Dixon, Brandon. 2017. "Faust Made $1.4 Million in 2015." *Harvard Crimson*, May 13. https://www.thecrimson.com/article/2017/5/13/tax-forms-2015/.

Flaherty, Colleen. 2018a. "Mental Health Crisis for Grad Students." *Inside Higher Ed*, Mar. 6. https://www.insidehighered.com/news/2018/03/06/new-study-says-graduate-students-mental-health-crisis.

———. 2018b. "A Very Mixed Record on Grad Student Mental Health." *Inside Higher Ed*, Dec. 6. https://www.insidehighered.com/news/2018/12/06/new-research-graduate-student-mental-well-being-says-departments-have-important.

Gale, Catharine R., G. David Batty, and Ian J. Deary. 2008. "Locus of Control at Age 10 Years and Health Outcomes and Behaviors at Age 30 Years: The 1970 British Cohort Study." *Psychosomatic Medicine* 70: 397–403.

Gerard, Leo. 2014. "Good People Don't Get Jobs." *Huffington Post*, Dec. 6. https://www.huffingtonpost.com/leo-w-gerard/good-people-dont-get-good_b_5935690.html.

Ginsberg, Benjamin. 2013. *The Fall of the Faculty*. Princeton: Princeton University Press.

Goodwin, Thomas H., and Raymond D. Sauer. 1995. "Life Cycle Productivity of Academic Research: Evidence from the Cumulative Histories of Academic Economists." *Southern Economic Journal* 61: 728–743.

Greenberg, Zoe. 2018. "What Happens to #MeToo When a Feminist Is the Accused." *New York Times*, Aug. 13. https://www.nytimes.com/2018/08/13/nyregion/sexual-harassment-nyu-female-professor.html.

Grey, Alex. 2017. "These Countries Have the Most Graduate Students." *World Economic Forum*. https://www.weforum.org/agenda/2017/02/countries-with-most-doctoral-graduates/.

Gross, Neil, and Solon Simmons. 2007. "The Social and Political Views of American Professors." Working Paper presented at Harvard University Symposium on Professors and Their Politics. https://citeseerx.ist.psu.edu/viewdoc/summary?doi=10.1.1.147.6141.

Herrmann, Rachel. 2016. "Imposter Syndrome Is Definitely a Thing." *Chronicle of Higher Education*, Nov. 16. https://www.chronicle.com/article/Impostor-Syndrome-Is/238418.

Hersch, J. 2014. "Catching Up Is Hard to Do: Undergraduate Prestige, Elite Graduate Programs, and the Earnings Premium." Vanderbilt Law and Economics Research Paper, nos. 14–23; Vanderbilt Public Law Research Paper, nos. 16–17. Available at SSRN: https://ssrn.com/abstract=2473238 or http://dx.doi.org/10.2139/ssrn.2473238.

Holley, John W. 1977. "Tenure and Research Productivity." *Research in Higher Education* 6: 181–192.

Hollis, Jack F., Christina M. Gullion, Victor J. Stevens, Phillip J. Brantley, Lawrence J. Appel, Jamy D. Ard, Catherine M. Champagne, et al. 2008. "Weight Loss during the Intensive Intervention Phase of the Weight-loss Maintenance Trial." *American Journal of Preventive Medicine* 35: 118–126.

Hurtado, Sylvia, Kevin Eagan, John Pryor, Hannah Whang, and Serge Tran. 2011. "Undergraduate Teaching Faculty: The 2010–2011 HERI Faculty Survey." Los Angeles: Higher Education Research Institute, UCLA.

Inbar, Yoel, and Joris Lammers. 2012. Political Diversity in Social and Personality Psychology. *Perspectives on Psychological Science* 7(5): 496–503.

Iyengar, Shanto, and Sean J. Westwood. 2015. "Fear and Loathing across Party Lines: New Evidence on Group Polarization." *American Journal of Political Science* 59: 690–707.

Jaschik, Scott. 2015. "Faculty Pay: Up and Uneven." *Inside Higher Ed*, Mar. 16. https://www.insidehighered.com/news/2015/03/16/survey -finds-increases-faculty-pay-and-significant-gaps-discipline.

Jenkins, Rob. 2016. "Community College Class FAQ: You Teach How Many Classes?" *Chronicle Vitae*, Oct. 25. https://chroniclevitae.com /news/1590-community-college-faq-you-teach-how-many-classes.

Kausel, Edgar E., Satoris S. Culbertson, and Hector P. Madrid. 2016. "Overconfidence in Personnel Selection: When and Why Unstructured Interview Information Can Hurt Hiring Decisions." *Organizational Behavior and Human Decision Processes* 137: 27–44.

Larson, Richard C., Navid Ghaffarzadegan, and Yi Xue. 2014. "Too Many PhDs or Too Few Academic Job Openings: The Basic Reproductive R_0 in Academia." *Systems Research and Behavioral Science* 31: 745–775.

Lewis, Lionel S. 1980. "Academic Tenure: Its Recipients and Its Effects." *Annals of the American Academy of Political and Social Science*. Vol 448, The Academic Profession, 86–101.

Lodge, Milton, and Charles Taber. 2013. *The Rationalizing Voter*. New York: Cambridge University Press.

MacFarquhar, Larissa. 2011. "How to Be Good." *New Yorker*, Sep. 5.

Magness, Phillip. 2016. "For-Profit Education and the Roots of Adjunctification in US Higher Education." *Liberal Education* 102. https://www .aacu.org/liberaleducation/2016/spring/magness.

McMahan, Jeff. 2017. "Derek Parfit (1942–2017)." *Philosophy Now*. https://philosophynow.org/issues/119/Derek_Parfit_1942-2017.

Munger, Michael. 2005. "Writing Your Dissertation and Creating Your Research Agenda." *Scaling the Ivory Tower*. Arlington, VA: Institute for Humane Studies.

Mutz, Diana. 2006. *Hearing the Other Side*. New York: Cambridge University Press.

Nerad, Maseri, Rebecca Aanerud, and Joseph Cerny. 1999. "So You Want to Become a Professor? Lessons from the PhDs—Ten Years Later Study." In *Paths to the Professoriate: Strategies for Enriching the Preparation of Future Faculty*, ed. Donald Wulff, Ann Austin, and Associates, 137–158. New York: Jossey-Bass.

Nordstrom, Susan Naomi, Amelie Nordstrom, and Coonan Nordstrom. 2018. "Guilty of Loving You: A Multispecies Narrative." *Qualitative Inquiry*, p.1077800418784321.

Okahana, Hironao, and Enyu Zhou. 2018. "Graduate Enrollment and Degrees: 2007 to 2017." Council of Graduate Schools. https://cgsnet.org/ckfinder/userfiles/files /CGS_GED17_Report.pdf.

O'Shaughnessy, Lynn. 2012. "Twelve Reasons Not to Get a PhD." *CBS News*, July 10. https://www.cbsnews.com/news/12-reasons-not-to-get-a-phd/.

Phillips, James Cleith. 2016. "Why Are There So Few Conservatives and Libertarians in Legal Academia? An Empirical Exploration of Three Hypotheses." *Harvard Journal of Law and Public Policy* 39: 153–208.

Pulakos, Elaine D., and Neal Schmitt. 1995. "Experience-based and Situational Interview Questions: Studies of Validity." *Personnel Psychology* 48: 289–308.

Read, Richard. 2015. "A $280 College Textbook Busts Budgets, but Harvard Author Gregory Mankiw Defends Royalties." *Oregonian*. https://www.oregonlive.com/education/2015/02/a_280_college _textbook_busts_b.html.

Rogers, Katrina. 2013. "Humanities Unbound: Supporting Careers and Scholarship beyond the Tenure Track." Charlottesville, VA: Scholarly Communication Institute, University of Virginia. http://katinarogers.com/wp-content/uploads /2013/08 /Rogers_SCI_Survey_ Report_09AUG13.pdf.

Rosenthal, Joel T. 1994. "The Work of Faculty: Expectations, Priorities, and Rewards." *Academe: The Bulletin of the AAUP* 80: 35–48.

Shields, Jon, and Joshua M. Dunn Sr. 2016. *Passing on the Right: Conservative Professors in the Progressive University*. New York: Oxford University Press.

Williams, Wendy, and Stephen Ceci. 2007. "Does Tenure Really Work?" *Chronicle of Higher Education* 53. https://www.chronicle.com/article /Does-Tenure-Really-Work-/25565.

Ziker, John. 2014. "The Long, Lonely Job of Homo Academicus." *Blue Review*, Boise State University, Mar. 31. http://thebluereview.org /faculty-time-allocation/.

INDEX

job advertisements, 121
job applications: CVs, 128-31;
  dossiers, 125-26; numbers, 124;
  time reviewed, 48-49; widely
  distributed, 121-22; writing well,
  126-28
job interviews, 122-23. *See also*
  interview questions
job market. *See* academic job
  market
job placements, 31-33, 54-56,
  119-20. *See also* academic jobs;
  jobs, getting
jobs, getting: advice (miscella-
  neous), 67-70; competition
  toward, 45-49; increasing
  difficulty, 55; institutional
  prestige's importance in, 52-56;
  networking's importance for,
  73-75; outside academia, 157-59;
  overview, 80; two-body
  problem, 72-73. *See also*
  academic job market
job security, 20, 21-22, 149-50
job shortage: practical implications, 147; supply vs. demand
  problem, 141-46; terminological
  problem, 141
journals, 39, 106, 115

knowledge, background, 103

labor theory of value, 65, 89
Lammars, Joris, 152
law professors, 152-53
learning, 41-42, 147-49
lecturers, 18
lecturing, 114-15
liberal arts colleges, 14-15
libertarians, 152-53
locus of control, 120
luck, 120

Magness, Phil, 30-31, 142
Mankiw, Greg, 30
marginal benefits, 86-88
marginal costs, 86-88

master's degrees, 58, 60
minorities, 110
Munger, Mike, 69-70, 96, 98-99

networking, 73-75
North, Douglass C., 98-99

office hours, 66
Olympics analogy, 45-46, 68
online education, 147-50
opportunity cost, 61

paid talks, 12
parenting, 63
Parfit, Derek, 82-83, 85
perfection, seeking, 75, 97
PhD degrees: cost, 59-61; necessity, 49; nonacademic uses,
  157-58; progression toward,
  57-59; purpose, 8-9. *See also* PhD
  programs
PhD programs: admission to,
  50-52, 60; difficulty of, 61-62;
  English, 56; hatred of, 64;
  incongruence with jobs, 9-10, 12;
  length of, 56-57, 77-79; placement of graduates, 54-55;
  quitting, 77; rank of, 52-56;
  reasons for entering, 7-8, 42-43;
  relative ease of, 62-64, 77;
  succeeding in, 1, 45-47, 57-59;
  tiers, 56; variation in, 52-53;
  volatility of, 54. *See also* rank of
  institution
PhD students: debt and, 60-61;
  demands on time, 90-91;
  emulating successful, 55, 68;
  income of, 57, 59-60;
  transformation into professors,
  47, 61-62
Phillips, James Cleith, 152-53
philosophy, 50, 53-54
physics research, 36-37
pitches, 131-32
presenting papers, 98-99
pressure, working under, 90
prestige, 51-56

teaching efficiency/effectiveness, 112–16

teaching fees, 23. *See also* salaries

teaching journals, 115

teaching load, 11, 13–16, 62–63, 112

teaching vs. publishing, 67, 71

tenure system: criteria, 19, 123, 140; firing, 18–19; process, 139; publish-or-perish aspect, 139–40; rationale/reality, 19–20; tenure as hire, 140–41; tenure review, 129

thinking via writing, 101–2

time budgets, 83–85, 91–92, 93, 109–10

time management, 102, 108–9

time of day, 91

Tomasi, John, 134

tuition, waiving, 59–60

undergraduate institutions, 51–52

undergraduates, 39–42, 147–48

unemployment, 157

unpleasant truths, 2–4

urgency vs. importance, 90–91, 108–9

visiting faculty, 24–25

vouching for talent, 108

wage premium, reasons for, 148–49

Westwood, Sean, 151–52

women, requests for service work, 110

work: balance with life, 83–85; endless, 81–82; under pressure, 90

work week, 11–16

writer's block, 101–2

writing: for the ages, 96–97; boring vs. good, 126–28; conveyor belt, 69–70; diminishing returns, 87; editing, 102; reading everything, 98–100; thinking, 101–2; time budget, 91–92. *See also* publishing

Zhuo, Daisy, 56